SANCTIFICATION

GORDON H. CLARK

The Trinity Foundation
Jefferson, Maryland

Cover: *The Finding of Moses*
Sebastien Bourdon
National Gallery of Art, Washington
Samuel H. Kress Collection

Sanctification
© 1992 John W. Robbins
The Trinity Foundation
Post Office Box 700
Jefferson, Maryland 21755
ISBN: 0-940931-33-8

Contents

Books by Gordon H. Clark

Readings in Ethics (1931)
Selections from Hellenistic Philosophy (1940)
A History of Philosophy (coauthor, 1941)
A Christian Philosophy of Education (1946, 1988)
A Christian View of Men and Things (1952, 1991)
What Presbyterians Believe (1956)[1]
Thales to Dewey (1957, 1989)
Dewey (1960)
Religion, Reason and Revelation (1961, 1986)
William James (1963)
Karl Barth's Theological Method (1963)
The Philosophy of Science and Belief in God (1964, 1987)
What Do Presbyterians Believe? (1965, 1985)
Peter Speaks Today (1967)[2]
The Philosophy of Gordon H. Clark (1968)
Biblical Predestination (1969)[3]
Historiography: Secular and Religious (1971)
II Peter (1972)[2]
The Johannine Logos (1972, 1989)
Three Types of Religious Philosophy (1973, 1989)
First Corinthians (1975, 1991)
Colossians (1979, 1989)
Predestination in the Old Testament (1979)[3]
I and II Peter (1980)
Language and Theology (1980)
First John (1980, 1992)
God's Hammer: The Bible and Its Critics (1982, 1987)
Behaviorism and Christianity (1982)
Faith and Saving Faith (1983, 1990)
In Defense of Theology (1984)
The Pastoral Epistles (1984)
The Biblical Doctrine of Man (1984, 1992)
The Trinity (1985, 1990)
Logic (1985, 1988)
Ephesians (1985)
Clark Speaks From the Grave (1986)
Logical Criticisms of Textual Criticism (1986, 1990)
First and Second Thessalonians (1986)
Predestination (1987)
The Atonement (1987)
The Incarnation (1988)
Today's Evangelism: Counterfeit or Genuine? (1990)
Essays on Ethics and Politics (1992)
Sanctification (1992)

[1] Revised in 1965 as *What Do Presbyterians Believe?*
[2] Combined in 1980 as *I & II Peter.*
[3] Combined in 1987 as *Predestination.*

Foreword

Many people in relatively orthodox churches are confused about sanctification. On the one hand, there are those whose views are summarized by the phrase, "Let go and let God." They tend to be generally Charismatic or Pentecostal. On the other hand, there are those who believe that justification is by grace, but sanctification is by works. They tend to be Reformed. These errors are common to human attempts at achieving salvation. Human religions divide into two groups, the mystics and the workers. Each group has chosen a wrong method of salvation and so fails to find it.

The Bible teaches that salvation, from start to finish, from election to glorification, from eternity to eternity, is all of grace. The great hymn writer, Augustus Toplady, expressed the Christian view of salvation when he wrote the words: "But not for works which we have done/Or shall hereafter do/Hath God decreed on sinful man/Salvation to bestow." Our works, both before and after regeneration, are not the basis or cause of our salvation. We are justified—declared legally righteous by God and pardoned from all sin—by grace alone through faith alone, apart from works. Furthermore, our justification is wholly *outside* of us; it is a work that God has done *for* us by imputing Christ's perfect righteousness to our account. It is not a work done *in* us by God.

Sanctification, however, is not done outside of us. It is a subjective moral change in our character that begins with regeneration and ends with our glorification in heaven. The thirteenth chapter of the Westminster Confession of Faith, "Of Santification," summarizes the Bible's teaching in these words:

> They, who are once effectually called, and regenerated, having a new heart, and a new spirit created in them, are further sanctified, really and personally, through the virtue of Christ's death and resurrection, by his Word and Spirit dwelling in them: the dominion of the whole body of sin is destroyed, and the several lusts thereof are more and more weakened and mortified; and they more and more quickened and strengthened in all saving graces, to the practice of true holiness, without which no man shall see the Lord.
>
> This sanctification is throughout in the whole man, yet imperfect in this life, there abiding still some remnants of corruption in every part; whence arises a continual and irreconcilable war, the flesh lusting against the Spirit, and the Spirit against the flesh.
>
> In which war, although the remaining corruption, for a time, may much prevail; yet, through the continual supply of strength from the sanctifying Spirit of Christ, the regenerate part does overcome; and so the saints grow in grace, perfecting holiness in the fear of God.

Both justification and sanctification are the work of God, not of ourselves; one work, justification, takes places wholly *outside* of us; the second, sanctification, is God's work in cleansing us from all sin. The Larger Catechism says that sanctification is "the work of God's free grace, whereby we are renewed in the whole man after the image of God, and are enabled more and more to die unto sin and live unto righteousness."

In short, men do not make themselves holy; neither their regeneration nor their growth in grace is due to their own diligence or obedience, but to God alone. The fruit of the Spirit—love, joy, peace, longsuffering, kindness, goodness, faithfulness, gentleness, self-control—are just that, the fruit of the Spirit, not of ourselves, for it is Christ who lives in us, and it is Christ who works in us both to will and to do his good pleasure. We are commanded to "work out" what God has already "worked in" us. We cannot work out unless God works in us, for without Christ we can do nothing. We are Christ's workmanship, not our own.

But *how* does God sanctify us? Is it simply, "let go and let God?" The Christian answer to this question, already expressed in the quotation from the Westminster Confession, may surprise some in this emotional and anti-intellectual age: God works through knowledge. Christ prayed, "Sanctify them by your *truth*; your word is truth." Peter prayed that "grace and peace be multiplied to you in the *knowledge* of God and of Jesus our Lord." The reason for his prayer is obvious: "His divine power has given to us all things that pertain to life and godliness through the *knowledge* of him who called us by glory and virtue, by which have been given to us exceedingly great and precious promises, that through these you may be partakers of the divine nature . . . ."

It is common in some religious circles to decry the futility of education in changing men's lives. Education, we are told, is the pagan Greek method, not the Christian method, of changing men. But such an attitude is far removed from the Bible. It is precisely education, education in the truth, that is the means of our sanctification. James tells us, "Of his own will he [God] brought us forth by the word of truth," for the "implanted word is able to save your souls." Christ is our Teacher, and we are sanctified by his knowledge.

That is why this book on sanctification so emphasizes Bible study. God sanctifies his people through his Word. Unless we know that Word, we cannot be sanctified. Our imperfect and sin-stained obedience to God's moral law, which is holy, just, and good, is not the cause of our sanctification, but the result. Unless we were already sanctified, we would find it in us neither to will nor to do God's will. Sanctification is not by works, lest any man should boast. Nor, on the other hand, do we "let go and let God" and in some mystical way become sanctified. It is our hope that this book will eliminate some of the confusion surrounding the doctrine of sanctification in the church today.

John W. Robbins
April 1992

Introduction

In colloquial Christian conversation the term *salvation* is very frequently misused. There is a story of a Salvation Army lassie in London who approached a man on the street and asked, Are you saved? The man happened to be an Anglican bishop. He replied to the question, Do you mean *sesōuenos, sēzomenos,* or *sōthesomenos?* Which being interpreted, means, have I been saved, am I being saved, or shall I be saved? Poor lassie. In plain English, salvation is a broad term that includes regeneration, justification, adoption, sanctification, and glorification. The present study concerns sanctification.

Regeneration is an act of God. By it he instantaneously produces an effect in man, a change in which man is totally passive. Jeremiah 13:23 puts it rather picturesquely: "Can the Ethiopian change his skin or the leopard his spots?" Co-temporaneously God does something else that is not a change in man at all. Justification is an instantaneous judicial act of acquittal. Sanctification, however, is neither instantaneous, nor is a man passive therein. It is not instantaneous because it is a time-consuming, subjective, life-long process. Nor is it an act of God alone. It is indeed dependent on the continuous power of God, but it is also the activity of the regenerated man. Both God and man are active. Sanctification *is* the Christian life.

Since the external conditions of individuals, and even more their mentality and psychological quirks, differ enormously, any descriptive account of the Christian life would bog down in multitudinous details. Nor can biography be normative. Scripture, however, gives some general principles. No matter how different Chinese Christians may be from American Christians, no matter how different two Christians of the same nationality are, we are all tempted, we all sin, we all grow in grace, and we all persevere, though by multiple methods, at various velocities, and to different degrees.

1. Conversion and Repentance

Since the term *sanctification* commonly refers to the life-long battle against sin, it is not usual to include regeneration in the concept. Regeneration initiates the Christian life, resurrecting the dry bones and clothing them with flesh—something only God can do—but the first conscious human activity in this new life is faith. Faith, human activity as it is, is still a gift from God. This activity, or its first moments, may be called conversion. The previous state of mind is replaced by belief in the atoning death of Christ. The man consciously changes his mind—for repentance is a change of mind—and turns from his old thinking toward the Savior. First Peter 2:25 reports concerning his addressees, who had been previously straying like lost sheep, that they had now returned to the Shepherd and Bishop of their souls. Acts 11:21 is less flowery, but more exact: "A great number believed and turned to the Lord." In theological language this turning is called *conversion*. The German pastor of the Presbyterian church at 19th and Susquehanna in Philadelphia, back in the 1920's, in the *Schlussversammlung* of an evangelistic series, dramatically illustrated it by executing an about face in the pulpit as he said, *"Bekehren ist umkehren."*

If, now, one wishes to examine what is simultaneous, or what the logical relations are, one could say that repentance itself, more commonly connected with aversion from sin than with belief in the Trinity, is an act of, and a part of, faith. Believing is indeed an act of the human self, caused by God to be sure, and totally impossible except for regeneration and God's gift; but it is nonetheless a human volition. It is the first act in a Christian life. Dead bones cannot believe; but when clothed with flesh they live, and they live a life of faith. By means of this volition God justifies the sinner on the ground of Christ's merits. This judicial pronouncement inevitably, if some people do not care to say automatically, sets in motion the life-long process of sanctification. The purpose of justification, or at least one of the purposes, and the immediate one, is to produce sanctification. The earliest stage of this is conversion, so early that it might be identified with the first act of faith itself. Consider some of the Scriptural material, both from the Old Testament and from the New Testament.

Psalm 19:7: The law of the Lord is perfect, converting the soul.

Psalm 51:13: Then will I teach transgressors thy ways, and sinners shall be converted unto thee.

Isaiah 6:10: Make the heart of this people fat . . . lest they understand with their heart and convert.

These three Old Testament verses indicate that turning to the Lord, or conversion, depends on understanding his laws. If a person does not understand, his fatty heart will not turn. But the New Testament gives more details as to the nature of the turning.

Matthew 13:15 has "This people's heart is waxed gross . . . and their eyes have they closed, lest at any time they . . . should understand with their heart and should be converted." (Compare Mark 4:12, John 12:40, and Acts 28:27.)

These four verses repeat Isaiah, to wit, that unless a person understands—not botany or mathematics, but theology—he cannot be converted. This idea has puzzled many Christians and has no doubt contributed to the prevalence of Arminianism. If the phrase "understand with their heart" is taken to mean faith, the conclusion will be that faith temporally precedes regeneration. But the verse says no such thing. First of all, note that God may, but need not, use means to accomplish his ends. Obviously creation *ex nihilo* could have no means. On the other hand, when God saved the Israelites from the pursuing Egyptians, he used a strong east wind. Now, God could omnipotently regenerate a man without using any means (if it should so please him), and in a sense he does so. But he has so ordered the situation that there are conditions. A condition preceding faith is an understanding of the propositions to be believed. No one can believe that of which he knows nothing. Saul, the persecutor, understood Christian doctrine better than the Christians did. The people referred to in Matthew 13:15 deliberately avoided an understanding, for fear that it might convert them. Hence understanding the gospel, at least understanding some of it, must precede regeneration alone as the east wind preceded the escape of the Israelites. But understanding alone is not faith. Faith is believing what one understands. A theologian or philosopher understands many theories he does not believe. In regeneration God causes the sinner to believe what heretofore he had only understood. As Paul said, "Faith cometh by hearing." This is the means God uses.

Consider also Luke 22:32: "Satan hath desired to have you, but . . . when thou hast turned again, strengthen thy brethren."

One may ask, Was Peter converted twice? Does not conversion occur only once? The answer is two-fold. First, the verb *to turn* is not a very precise term. Repentance is a more exact one. Second, many people backslide. They turn away from the Lord, succumb to temptation, and, like David, turn again to the Lord. Some popular expressions in modern times give the impression that conversion, like regeneration, occurs only once. Thus because *conversion* is a flexible word, it is better to consider repentance. Repentance too can be misunderstood, but even its colloquial use does not tie it so strictly to a momentary occurrence. The exposition therefore requires other verses, one of which bears directly on the connection between conversion and repentance.

Acts 3:19: Repent therefore and turn again . . . .

Matthew 4:17: Repent, for the kingdom is at hand.

Acts 5:31: To give repentance to Israel and forgiveness of sins.

Revelation 2:5: . . . except thou repent.

In the New Testament there are about sixty instances of the noun and the verb. The first one quoted above relates repentance to conversion. The chronological sequence seems to be that a sinner changes his mind and then turns to God. But, after all, changing one's mind (in this context) is itself turning to God. *Repentance* is to be taken literally, while *turning* is a figure of speech. The other verses do not so explicitly relate conversion to repentance. The nature of the latter shows it to be, not so much identical to conversion, as inclusive of it. Conversion therefore may be considered as the first phase of faith and repentance. These two, faith and repentance, as one and the same, are intellectual life and action. This might not have been guessed from the verb *to turn*. But the verb *repent* is explicitly to *change one's mind*. It is the replacement of a totally secular set of ideas by at least a few Christian propositions. The first act of replacement may be momentary as an initial act; but the replacement is permanent.

One continues to believe in the lordship and the resurrection of Christ forever—as the doctrine of perseverance will soon show. But the replacement of secular and erroneous ideas with Biblical doctrines continues in a life-long process. Newly born Christians, in varying degrees, inevitably become better theologians as time goes on.

The people who will read this book will probably be divided into two groups, perhaps not sharply separated, but in various degrees interested in one phase of the discussion more than another. One of those groups may view the other as only superficially interested in sanctification, willing to dabble in theory because of curiosity but not much interested in the personal and practical increase of holiness. These latter may view the so-called practical Christians as well meaning, but only superficially and unintelligently committed to Christianity. As thus more sharply contrasted than the continuum justifies, both groups have blundered. The two ends of the spectrum have blundered the most; the center may be well adjusted. Since, however, the non-theoretical and non-theological group would be more inclined to pick up a book on sanctification, it may be proper here, almost at the beginning, to point out a very clear directive to holiness. The very few pages to this point should show the indispensability of studying the Scriptures. No doubt the Christian who wants to be a better Christian should pay his debts promptly and do an errand for his sick neighbor, but he learns such duties and others more important only by studying the Bible. Ezekiel 25 and Revelation 16 may not tell anyone what to do this afternoon, but eighteen months from now, or seven years from now, they will be precisely what is needed. Hence the first indispensable step after regeneration is Bible study. Theology is the road to holiness.

While it is important to note that repentance is a

continuous and life-long change of mind, rather than a momentary emotional upheaval, it is equally necessary to characterize the new ideas by which the mind is changed. Obviously it is not a change from believing that the Dodgers will win the World Series to the belief that the New York Yankees will. An excellent statement of the change of mind required is given in the *Westminster Shorter Catechism*.

> Repentance unto life is a saving grace, whereby a sinner out of a true sense of his sin, and apprehension of the mercy of God in Christ, doth, with grief and hatred of his sin, turn from it unto God, with full purpose of, and endeavor after, new obedience.

Some further verses are

> Jeremiah 31:19: . . . turn thou to me, and I shall be turned; for thou art the Lord my God. Surely after that I was turned, I repented; and after that I was instructed, I smote upon my thigh; I was ashamed, yea, even confounded, because I did not bear the reproach of my youth.
>
> Luke 1:77-79: To give knowledge of salvation unto his people by the remission of their sins, through the tender mercy of our God; whereby the dayspring from on high hath visited us. To give light to them that sit in darkness and in the shadow of death, to guide our feet into the way of peace.
>
> Acts 2:37, 38: Now when they heard this, they were pricked in their heart, and said unto Peter and to the rest of the apostles, Men and brethren, what shall we do? Then Peter said unto them, Repent, and be baptized every one of you in the name of Jesus Christ for the remission of sins, and ye shall receive the gift of the Holy Ghost.

Romans 6:18: Being made free from sin, ye became the servants of righteousness.

II Corinthians 7:10: For godly sorrow worketh repentance to salvation not to be repented of; but the sorrow of the world worketh death.

The verse in Jeremiah shows that the act of turning from sin to God is one that God himself causes. Or, as another verse says, it is a grant or gift from God, for Peter in Acts 11:18 concluded, "Then hath God also to the Gentiles granted repentance unto life." It cannot be too greatly emphasized that repentance, the change of mind, is produced by God. We are indeed conscious of some change; we are aware that once we did not believe in sin and salvation and now we do; but Bible study will teach us that God caused the change. Repentance is a gift.

The verse in Luke also states that the knowledge of salvation is a gift from God; and in addition it indicates the blessings of salvation in contrast with the darkness of sin and the shadow of death. Thus each verse adds one or more ideas to the explanation of repentance.

The religious world of the present century has witnessed a tidal wave of anti-intellectualism. Inundated by the outright irrationalism of the neo-orthodox and the existentialists, popular religion holds every intellectual decision—the acceptance of an intellectual doctrine—to be either insincere or trivial, and that only emotion is genuine and "authentic." With the prevalence of such views, a further repetition of the Catechism seems called for. Repentance includes an "apprehension of the mercy of God in Christ." Before regeneration a sinful human being does not think this way. He believes that God is too good to condemn anybody, and, besides, he himself is quite respectable. But the gift of faith changes his ideas. Jesus, whom he previously admitted to be an admirable ethical teacher, he now believes to be the Lord of Glory. The sins he has loved, he now hates, or at least begins to hate, for regeneration is not instantaneous perfection. By this change of mind he turns from sin to God; or, more accurately, this change of mind *is* his turning to God. Nor can this turning or conversion occur without a full purpose and endeavor to obey God's law. There is nothing insincere in this. To use John Calvin's remark, it is the pious assent of the mind.

Repentance, not just its initial phase, but as a life-long state of mind, is to be further explained by the doctrine of the perseverance of the saints; but the points already made can be accentuated by contrast with aberrant theories; after which perseverance will fall into place.

2. Aberrant Theories

Pelagius

Pelagius, a British monk about A.D. 400, of all the professedly Christian writers before the twentieth century, sponsored the most extreme and most unbiblical theories of regeneration and conversion. Now, an aberrant theory of regeneration logically affects the account of grace, the atonement, and all other doctrines. Thus Pelagius affirmed free will and denied depravity. The idea of repentance must be altered as well, and so also sanctification. Not only does a wrong principle logically affect the entire body of theology proceeding from it, but, further, there are historical effects. Augustine in his defense of grace prevented the western church from becoming entirely Pelagian, but it became semi-Pelagian nonetheless. Then in modern times Arminius turned back, perhaps more than he realized, from Reformation Calvinism to the semi-Pelagianism of Rome. Hence Pelagius still influences theology today.

Reformation theology holds that Adam was created positively righteous. Not only does Genesis 1:27 pellucidly imply as much, but Ephesians 4:24 and Colossians 3:10 repeat it. This makes Adam's fall difficult to understand. How could a man created righteous have even been tempted, not to mention succumbing to it? Some theologians simply say that Adam was created righteous but mutable. This begs the question. How could one perfectly righteous, and therefore without evil desires, be mutable so as to sin? Many theologians avoid the problem. H.B. Smith concludes that it is insoluble. A.H. Strong (*Systematic Theology* Vol. II, pp. 585ff.) briefly describes about a dozen attempts, but he himself offers no explanation. It seems to me that supralapsarianism is the only answer. Otherwise one must be content to say merely that Romanism's solution is even worse than those of the theologians mentioned. Romanism holds that man was created morally neutral, but then God gave Adam an extra gift of righteousness. This hardly makes sin any more understandable. Whether the righteousness was original or a later gift has no bearing on the matter. The paradox is how a perfectly righteous being could sin. The same problem occurs with the initial sin of the now fallen angels. Pelagius simply held that Adam was created morally neutral: *ut sine virtute, ita sine vitio, i.e.,* neither virtuous nor sinful. His body was mortal, and physical death was not and is not a punishment for sin. Since Adam had no original righteousness to restrain him, Pelagius easily explains sin on the basis of free will.

Since this view conceives of sin as nothing other than a voluntary transgression of the law, Adam's sin could not in itself injure his posterity, nor affect their free will—naturally, because a *free* will is one that cannot be affected. Therefore at birth every infant is in the same state as Adam was at creation. There is no original sin or inherent corruption. Julian, a disciple of Pelagius, wrote, "Nothing in man is sin, if nothing is of his own volition or assent. . . . No one is naturally evil." On this view sin cannot be inherited, and to us Adam is only a bad example.

After having taught several thousand college students over a period of sixty years, I am aware, not only of a lack of historical information on their part, but, worse, of a disinterest in history. Many of these students retain this disinterest for the remainder of their lives. Therefore, if they are church-goers, they dislike sermons which explain the views of antiquated theologians. What they fail to note is that these antiquated views are very modern. With hardly an exception the sects repeat the ancient heresies.

One of Pelagius's basic propositions, repeated in modern times by Immanuel Kant, was that "ability limits obligation." Man must have plenary ability to do whatever God can righteously require of him. If God commands, "Thou shalt love the Lord thy God with all thy heart, and with all thy soul, and with all thy mind, and with all thy strength," then every man has complete ability to obey the command perfectly. Man has free will. This theory of plenary ability was not only adopted by Immanuel Kant and many secular thinkers; it was also the basis of John Wesley's doctrine of sinless perfection. Neither God nor sin can limit free will.

The besetting sin of false theology, if it professes to be somewhat Christian, is the substitution of incorrect definitions for the Biblical definitions. In this case an important example is the term *sin*. One must constantly keep in mind that sin, for Pelagius, is not "any want of conformity unto," but only voluntary "transgression of the law of God." Children are not born in iniquity; they remain innocent until they voluntarily disobey a divine law. They are not guilty of Adam's sin; neither are adults. Adam is not our federal head, nor can God impute either sin or righteousness to anyone except the individual voluntary agent. Each must pass his own probation, as the neo-orthodox also say. God would be the "author of sin" unless a man is condemned or justified solely on the ground of his own individual conduct.

Augustine made a crushing reply: Why, then, does the Church baptize infants? As a matter of fact, Pelagius answered this question by saying that infants are baptized in order to wash away their future sins; but Augustine's question had its effect because Pelagius's answer was so clearly contrary to the view held throughout the Church.

At any rate, Pelagius admitted that most if not all adults have sinned. What then is to be done? First, baptism, as just reported, cleanses a man of his sins. But, second, the man must "repent" and decide to keep the law of God perfectly. That it is possible to keep the law perfectly is evident from the fact that past sins, past voluntary transgressions, cannot bind a free will. Then, third, God does not command the impossible. Ability limits responsibility. Repentance is therefore a decision never to sin again. Not only does Pelagius make a place for repentance, he can even speak of grace—he can call grace unmerited favor; but the favor is not the irresistible action of the Spirit on our minds and wills. For Pelagius "grace" consists of (1) the natural freedom of the will; (2) the revelation of God's law; and (3) the remission of sins by baptism. Thus all men can, and many who know God's revelation do, live without sin.

Augustine vigorously attacked Pelagianism; but his victory was neither complete nor enduring. In the fifth century Pelagianism or an inconsistent semi-Pelagianism spread through southern France. This was combatted by a decree of the sixth century Council of Orange—to be quoted after noting that by the ninth century Calvinism had only the feeble voice of the martyr Gottschalk. The decree declares

If anyone assert that by reason of man's prayer the grace of God is conferred, but that it is not grace itself which causes that God is prayed to, he contradicts the prophet Isaiah (65:1), and the Apostle Paul (Romans 10:20) saying the same thing, "I was found of them that sought me not and have been manifest unto them that asked not after me." If anyone maintain that God waits for a willingness in us to be purged of sin, and does not allow that the very willingness to be cleansed of sin is wrought in us by the infusion and operation of the Holy Ghost, he resists the Holy Ghost, saying with Solomon, "The will is prepared by the Lord," and with the apostle, "It is God which worketh in you both to will and to do of his good pleasure" (Philippians 2:13).

This is an excellent statement of the Calvinistic position and shows that the Biblical doctrine was still professed by a good portion of the visible church. God does not wait for a willingness on the part of the sinner before purging him of his sin. The will is not free, for God works in us "both to will" as well as "to do," and his working is of his own good pleasure. But this pure gospel was soon to be obscured in the night of superstition.

Council of Trent

Romish views of repentance, or penance, now follow historically before more modern views are considered. Augustine had vigorously attacked Pelagius and secured his condemnation. He defended a view of grace which one can at the very least call far more Biblical than Pelagius's view. In later life he dropped his own earlier, not-so-extreme, theory of free will and wrote forthrightly on predestination. But as he was writing, the barbarians sacked Rome and ushered in four centuries of anarchy and ignorance. The utter anarchy was fairly well eliminated by

Charlemagne, but with his death ignorance continued and superstition increased until the Protestant Reformation. It was during these centuries that Augustine's theology was obscured; and the official position of Romanism was finally formulated by the Council of Trent. This position is not Pelagianism: that much of Augustine remained. But it has been and is properly called semi-Pelagianism. What then is the Romish doctrine of repentance, or, more exactly, penance, a sacrament which they substitute for Scriptural repentance?

In the first place Romanists believe in baptismal regeneration. By the intention of the priest the holy water regenerates the infant. This has one distressing consequence. Since it is the intention of the priest that validates the baptism, the parents can never be sure that their child has been baptized. No doubt priests almost without exception have the right intention. But there was one who confessed that for some years he had baptized, or better, gone through the motions and the formula, intending to damn the child. This may be a unique exception; but it is possible that several other priests had simply not intended what the church intends. Hence these infants were not baptized validly and so not regenerated. A valid baptism, however, is supposed to remove all sin. The Council of Trent, Sixth Session (January 13, 1547) decided:

> The instrumental cause [of justification] is the sacrament of baptism. . . . He maketh us just . . . (chapter VII). No one ought to make use of that rash saying . . . that the observance of the commandments of God is impossible for the one who is justified, for God does not command impossibilities. . . . From which it is plain that they are opposed to the orthodox doctrine of religion who assert that the just man sins, venially at least, in every good work . . ." (chapter XI; compare also Canon XXV).

The Reformed doctrine is that although some sins are more heinous than others, none is "venial," but all are deadly in that they all deserve the wrath and curse of God. That baptism makes us actually just before God, and that, at least sometimes, we do not sin even venially in our good works, is bad enough. But what is worse, Romanism also teaches that a sinner can do more than God requires of him. These so-called works of supererogation are deposited in the Treasury of the Saints and are later issued, by order of the Pope, to other sinners who have not done enough. In this way Rome teaches that although Christ's sacrifice is necessary to salvation, it is not sufficient. Additional human merits must be added.

The distribution of these extra merits and the forgiveness of sin now depend on the Romish substitute for repentance, namely the sacrament of penance. Canon VI says,

> If anyone denieth either that sacramental confession was instituted or is necessary to salvation, of divine right; or saith that the manner of confessing secretly to a priest alone . . . is alien from the institution and commands of Christ, and is a human invention, let him be anathema.

Canon IX continues,

> If anyone saith that the sacramental absolution of the priest is not a judicial act, but a bare ministry of pronouncing and declaring sins to be forgiven . . . let him be anathema.

Canon XII also:

> If anyone saith that God always remits the whole punishment together with the guilt, and that the

satisfaction of penitents is no other than the faith whereby they apprehend that Christ has satisfied for them, let him be anathema.

Canon XIII:

If anyone saith that satisfaction for sins, as to their temporal punishment, is nowise made to God, through the merits of Jesus Christ, by the punishments inflicted by him . . . or by those enjoined by the priest, nor even by those voluntarily undertaken, as by fastings, prayers, alms-deeds, or by other works also of piety, and that therefore the best penance is merely a new life, let him be anathema.

The Council of Trent, sitting off and on for several years after Luther's death, produced these formulations. But their substance had been in effect for some centuries. The young Luther in all his piety sought holiness and sanctification by the only methods he knew. But he was always apprehensive that he had not done enough, had not fasted enough, had not flagellated himself enough, not earned enough merits for salvation. As a professor of theology he studied Paul's epistle to the Romans, and as a very intelligent scholar he began to understand the Scripture as contrasted with Romish superstition. He then discarded the medieval methods of sanctification and adopted what for his age was an unknown doctrine. He started to preach what Trent so definitely condemned.

Note that these Canons assert the necessity of sacramental confession to a priest secretly; that the priest's absolution is not "ministerial and declarative" as the Protestants hold, but a "judicial act;" and finally note again that Christ's satisfaction is not sufficient, but that to the work of Christ we must add punishments enjoined by a priest, plus the greater merit of voluntary fastings, *et cetera.*

No orthodox Protestant would deny that repentance requires an amendment of life—this is surely the doctrine of sanctification—nor that it requires restitution when restitution is possible. But (1) in most cases no restitution is possible, and (2) when there is, our sins are not forgiven for the sake of other good works, nor for whatever temporal punishments God may inflict; but our sins are forgiven on the basis of Christ's merits alone. Augustus Toplady may have been thinking mainly of justification at the time, but what he wrote covers the whole Christian life:

> But not for works which we have done,
> Or shall hereafter do,
> Hath God decreed on sinful man
> Salvation to bestow.

The Papal system, however, claims to earn merits by penance.

The wording of the Council of Trent is of course definitive and authoritative. It is interesting, however, and instructive to read a recent statement from a Romish Dictionary on "Grace." Under the heading of "Penance" it says:

> i. Penitence, or repentance, a virtue disposing a sinner to hatred of his own sin. . . . It is a necessary condition of forgiveness.
> ii. Public. [some history of the early church to the XVIII century.]
> iii. Canonical. Prayers and good works, e.g. fasting, almsgiving, pilgrimage, retreat, imposed by ecclesiastical authority . . . either instead of or in order to obtain release from, a penalty.
> iv. Sacramental. After hearing a penitent's confes-

sion and before giving him absolution, a confessor must impose a penance. . . .

Then also, "Penance, the Sacrament of. A sacrament of the New Law instituted by Christ in which by the absolution of a priest, acting as judge, sins committed after Baptism are forgiven to a person who confesses them with sorrow and a purpose of amendment. . . ." And there follows a quotation from Trent.

With respect to the sorrow for and hatred of sin, referred to above, the Romanists speak of perfect contrition, by which sin is forgiven even before Penance, "though the obligation of confession remains." But since few people experience perfect contrition, there is an imperfect contrition, called "attrition," lesser in value, but "necessary and sufficient for the valid reception of the sacrament of Penance." Thus the action of a priest is a substitute for New Testament repentance.

John Wesley

Arminianism, in the person of John Wesley, who was neither a profound nor precise theologian, seems to have had a doctrine of two types of repentance. Wesley's second type may be more in accord with Scripture, but the first is without Scriptural support. In one place, speaking of faith and justification, he says, "God for the sake of his Son pardoneth and absolveth him who had in him, till then, no good thing. Repentance, indeed, God had given him before, but that repentance was neither more nor less than a deep sense of the want of all good and the presence of all evil."*

Note carefully what this says. Before God pardons a man, there is no good thing in him. Repentance was in him

---

* *John Wesley,* edited by Albert C. Outler (Oxford University Press, 1964), p. 205.

prior to his pardon. Therefore repentance is no good thing, even though it was a gift from God. Any theory of holiness based on such confusion can be no good thing.

Instead of pursuing the term repentance, however, it is easier to follow what Wesley said about faith, perseverance, and entire sanctification. The complex of ideas will show that even if he sometimes uses the term *repentance* in a more Scriptural manner, the whole is incompatible with perseverance and free grace, and therefore constitutes an aberrant theory of sanctification.

In the *Doctrinal Summaries* of the second annual conference in Bristol, on August 2, 1745, the following questions and answers were formulated (*op. cit.*, p. 150):

> Q. 12. Can faith be lost but through disobedience?
> A. It cannot. A believer first inwardly disobeys. . . . Then his intercourse with God is lost, *i.e.*, and after this [he is] like unto another man.
> Q. 13. How can such a man recover faith?
> A. By repenting and doing the first works.

The Lutherans as well as the Arminians teach that a regenerated person can nullify his regeneration. Mueller (*Christian Dogmatics*, p. 354) writes,

> It is clear doctrine of Scripture that believers in Christ may fall from grace or lose their faith, Luke 8:13, 14; I Tim. 1:19. This is proved also by the examples of David and Peter. This truth must be emphasized over against the Calvinists, who affirm that believers, when committing mortal sins, lose indeed the exercise of faith, but not faith itself.*

---

* The term *exercise* here is too vague to determine whether this is a correct statement of Calvinism.

But let us continue with the Arminians.

Since Wesley says that the believer may through disobedience lose his faith and his intercourse with God, and can only recover his faith by that "evil" repentance and first works, Wesley must, if consistent, assert that a man once regenerated can nonetheless fail to arrive in heaven and on the contrary be eternally lost in hell. If he is not to be lost, it appears that he must be regenerated a second time. Scripture contains no such idea. Regeneration initiates an everlasting life.

Calvinistic perseverance versus Wesleyan sinlessness is the main point in this discussion of sanctification, but first here is Wesley's reference to Calvinism made the same day.

> Q. 23. Wherein may we come to the very edge of Calvinism?
> A. 1. In ascribing all good to the free grace of God.[!]
> 2. In denying all natural free will and all power antecedent to grace. And 3. In excluding all merit from man, even for what he has or done by the grace of God.

With respect to sanctification more precisely, the formulations of Wednesday, June 17, 1747, were:

> Q. 1. How much is allowed by our brethren who differ from us with regard to entire sanctification? . . . But what do we allow them?
> A. We grant: 1. That many of those who have died in the faith . . . were not sanctified throughout . . . till a little before death. 2. That the term "sanctified" is continually applied by Paul to all that were justified. . . . 4. That consequently it is not proper to use it in that sense [saved from all sin] without adding the word "wholly," "entirely," or the like. . . .
> Q. 3. What then is the point wherein we divide?

A. It is this: whether we should expect to be saved from all sin before the article of death?

Q. 4. Is there any clear Scripture promise of this —that God will save us from all sin?

A. There is. "And he shall redeem Israel from all his iniquities," Psalm 130:8. "Then I will sprinkle clean water upon you, and ye shall be clean; from all your filthiness, and from all your idols, will I cleanse you . . . . I will also save you from all your uncleannesses: and I will call for the corn, and will increase it, and lay no famine upon you," Ezekiel 36:25, 29. "Having therefore these promises, dearly beloved, let us cleanse ourselves from all filthiness of the flesh and spirit, perfecting holiness in the fear of God," II Corinthians 7:1.

In the following Question and Answer he quotes:

"He that committeth sin is of the devil; for the devil sinneth from the beginning. For this purpose the Son of God was manifested, that he might destroy the works of the devil," I John 3:8; "Husbands, love your wives, even as Christ also loved the church, and gave himself for it; . . . that he might present it to himself a glorious church, not having spot, or wrinkle, or any such thing; but that it should be holy and without blemish," Ephesians 5:25, 27; and "For what the law could not do, in that it was weak through the flesh, God sending his own Son, condemned sin in the flesh; that the righteousness of the law might be fulfilled in us, who walk not after the flesh, but after the Spirit," Romans 8:3, 4.

Q. 6. Does the new Testament afford any further ground for expecting to be saved from all sin?

A. Undoubtedly it does. "And lead us not into temptation, but deliver us from evil," Matthew 6:13; "And the very God of peace sanctify you wholly; and I pray God your whole spirit and soul and body be preserved blameless unto the coming of our Lord

Jesus Christ," I Thessalonians 5:23; also John 17: 10-23
and Ephesians 3:14, 16-19. . . . Prayers for entire
sanctification, were there no such thing, would be a
mockery of God. . . .

Q. 9. But how does it appear that this is to be done
before death?

A. First, from the very nature of the command,
which is not given to the dead but unto the living.

He then quotes Titus 2:11-14 and Luke 1:69-75.

The significance of all these verses must not be passed
over in silence; but before their consideration it is well to
record Wesley's rejection of some points on which he was
misunderstood.

On Tuesday, August 15, 1758, the formulation was: "Q.
Did you affirm that perfection excludes all infirmities,
ignorance, and mistake? A. We continually affirm just the
contrary." And a few lines below he adds, "Everyone may
mistake [*ital.* his] as long as he lives."

However, to continue with Wesley's ideas and exact
words. He explains that perfection does not mean perfect
complete knowledge or omniscience; nor does it rule out
incorrect interpretations of the Scripture—even blatant
heresy?—"nor can we expect till then after death to be
wholly free from temptation. Such perfection belongeth
not to this life. . . . But if you would infer [from David's and
Abraham's sins] that all Christians do and must commit sin
as long as they live, this consequence we utterly deny" (*op.
cit.*, pp. 254, 257, 260).

Wesley argues at length that it is invalid to infer from
the fact of David's sin, of Peter's denial, or of other apostles'
sins, that no one can attain sinlessness before death.
Wesley is clearly correct in labeling such arguments
fallacies: "The holiest men among the Jews did sometimes
commit sin." No one need demur at his pointing out the
fallacy. The inference is indeed invalid; but this does not

mean that the conclusion should be denied. A conclusion can be true for some other reason than the silly premise of a stupid syllogism. For example, All dogs are vertebrates; George Washington crossed the Delaware; therefore David wrote the twenty-third Psalm. Obviously the conclusion does not follow from the premises. A reverse example is: All the heroes of Homer's *Iliad* died young; Alexander was a hero of Homer's *Iliad;* therefore Alexander died young. Here two *false* premises *validly* imply a *true* conclusion. To be a good theologian, one must know how to use syllogisms.

The last quotation from Wesley was made for the purpose of showing that Wesley affirms the possibility and the actuality of some men's achieving entire sinlessness before death. He relies on John's words, "he that is born of God sinneth not;" and he emphasizes "their plain, natural, and obvious meaning." But he fails to notice that this plain, natural, and obvious meaning would guarantee sinless perfection to every Christian from the moment of his regeneration on. John did not restrict his statement to a few octogenarian saints. He speaks to all his Christian readers. Wesley merely remarks that John did not contradict himself when he also said, "If we say we have no sin, we deceive ourselves," because even the man who has attained sinless perfection sinned earlier in life. Then he adds, "We fix his conclusion: a Christian is so far perfect as not to commit sin." If this were so, then Wesley was not a Christian when he wrote these words.

This raises the question whether Wesley had a correct idea of sin. It is hard to see how he can accommodate David's declaration, "I was shapen in iniquity and in sin did my mother conceive me." This does not refer to adultery on his mother's part. It means that David was guilty of sin before he was born. But aside from any rejection of original sin, though one must insist on its implications for overt sinful acts, Wesley seems deficient on these too. Can no "mistake" be sinful? Of course the Calvinist holds that a mistake in arithmetic is a noetic effect of sin. Are not all mistakes such? Ignorance *per se* need not be sin, for God has not revealed all truth to us; but are not mistakes in understanding Scripture sin? The Calvinist does not limit sin to voluntary transgressions. He holds that "any want of conformity unto" as well as any "transgression of the law of God" is sin. Wesley's view of sin is essentially Romish. Maybe even worse if he insists that there is no inherited guilt.

In this argument it is interesting to see Wesley relying on the "plain, natural, and obvious meaning" of John's words, and then to note his attack on Calvinism, where he rejects the plain and obvious meaning of "elect from the foundation of the world" and revises it to "they were not actually elect, or believers, till many ages after, in their several generations" (*Predestination Calmly Considered*, XVIII).

Wesley must also understand Romans 7 as a description of Paul's early life, which therefore has no bearing on his later life or on the achievements of other Christians. But Romans 6, 7, and 8 are not a mere personal biography of Paul. They answer the antinomian objections of the Pharisees, and thus they are a statement about the Christian life as such. If Romans 7 seems to be disheartening, one ought to remember that the chapter divisions are not in the manuscripts, and that Romans 7:25 and 8:1ff. are its conclusion.

Note that Romans 7:22 could be said only of a regenerated person. The man here delights in the law of God, and further the phrase "the inward man" rather clearly suggests "the new man" of other verses. Then too, the war described, with the armor of Ephesians 6:11ff., can only occur in a Christian life. Finally the man himself, Paul the apostle, thanks God for a future deliverance and a present "no condemnation." This cannot be the case of one who enjoys only a "no-good" repentance.

It is now time to consider the passages which Wesley uses to defend his doctrine of sinless perfection. There were four groups of these given in the preceding quotations. The first group was: Psalm 130:8, "He will redeem Israel from all his iniquities." Ezekiel 36:24-25, "I will take you from the nations . . . and bring you into your own land. Then will I sprinkle clean water upon you and you will be clean; I will cleanse you from all your filthiness and from all your idols. . . ." II Corinthians 7:1, "Let us cleanse ourselves from all defilements of flesh and spirit, perfecting holiness in the fear of God."

It should be evident to everyone that Psalm 130:8 does not promise sinless perfection before death. Any true Christian, even while at a deplorably low degree of sanctification, can say truly that God has redeemed me from all my iniquities. He has been bought by the blood of Christ and is redeemed. Even if an Arminian object to such a strong statement, and if he wants to equate redemption with sinless perfection, the verse does not say "in this life, before the article of death." The verse is a prediction of the future and not a statement of a past or present fact.

The passage in Ezekiel can and most probably does refer to the return of the dispersed Jews to their own land. If this be so, it holds out no promise of sinless perfection to Gentiles. Nor does it clearly promise sinless perfection to any Jew. Whatever it promises, it promises to the whole nation, and surely the Jews were not all sinless from 400 B.C. to A.D. 30. The most obvious reference is to the cessation of idolatry. Considering the history of the era, it can scarcely mean much more.

The third passage is addressed to the Christians at Corinth, and by implication to all other Christians. It is an exhortation to cleanse ourselves of all defilement. Wesley thinks it would be deceit or fraud for God to command anything impossible for us to accomplish. The Shorter Catechism says, "No mere man since the fall is able in this life perfectly to keep the commandments of God, but doth daily break them in thought, word, and deed." Romans 3:9, 10 and 8:8; Galatians 5:17; and I John 1:8 are all accurately reflected in the Catechism. If not, then God never imposed any commandments on the unregenerate, and if there is no law, there can be no condemnation, so that the unregenerate are automatically sinless.

God commits no fraud in commanding the impossible. Must Calvinism insist that Paul should have said, "Cleanse yourselves of all defilement except x, y, and z"? We are to perfect our holiness as a student of French tries to *perfectionner son francais*. But of course Wesley argues, as did Pelagius before him, that since ability limits responsibility, perfection does not require an American tongue to pronounce French perfectly. Such a maxim conflicts with the doctrine of total depravity and the fact that the unregenerate man is dead in sin and utterly unable to do any spiritual good. The only way Wesley can apply the commandments to sinners is to assert their ability to please God. But the Scriptures say that without faith it is impossible to please God; and yet the unregenerate is under obligation to keep the commandments. It has already been mentioned, and it will become clearer later on, that Wesley minimizes the seriousness of sin by his lack of ability to speak French.

The second group of verses Wesley uses to defend sinless perfection is: I John 3:8, "For this purpose the Son of God was manifested, that he might destroy the works of the devil." Ephesians 5:25, 27, ". . . as Christ also loved the church . . . that he might present it to himself . . . having no spot or wrinkle . . . holy and blameless."

Without quoting Romans 8:3, 4 we may note the confusion of mind that plagues Wesley in his use of these two passages. If I John 3:8 teaches sinless perfection before death, in that the works of the devil shall be destroyed, then the perfect Christian should not die. Death is the work of the devil, and, with the grave, is to be thrown into the lake of fire. Death is the last enemy to be destroyed. Therefore if Christ is to destroy the works of the devil, without exception, death must also be destroyed before we die. As said before, Wesley was not a very profound thinker.

The same type of reply applies also to his use of Ephesians 5:25, 27. Aside from the fact that the reference is rather clearly to an eschatological future, its application to the present age would imply that all the members of the church are to have no spot or wrinkle and be holy and blameless in the present age. This implies that Calvinists are not in the church and that Arminians are all perfect. Similarly, if Ephesians 3:16-19 imply sinlessness before death, they would also imply a veritable deification—all the fulness of God—and that too in the present life.

There is one more point. Arminians sometimes use Hebrews 6:4-6 to prove their theory of losing eternal life. Here are some persons who were once enlightened and had been made partakers of the Holy Ghost, but who have now fallen away. A Calvinist may try to understand "enlightened" and "partaker" in some external sense, such that a not too vicious sinner, attending church through custom, is restrained from grosser sins. But more likely the Calvinist will maintain that verse nine shows the passage to be, in grammatical terminology, a condition contrary to fact. At any rate, if this were not so, the Arminian still can take no pleasure in the passage, for whereas Wesley says that the fallen man must repent over again and repeat the first works, this passage says it is impossible for such people to renew themselves to repentance.

If the student wishes to examine the many other passages Wesley uses, he would do well to consult a half dozen commentaries. He will find that the same general type of reply as made here can be applied to them also. However, the subject is not yet exhausted, for the Bible teaches perseverance. This is the positive side of which the negative was the rejection of repetitive regenerations and sinless perfection.

3. Bishop Ryle and Assurance

The discussion now begins to become complex. In opposition to Wesleyanism, one could launch into the doctrine of perseverance. But this doctrine is also an answer, or at least a partial answer to questions about assurance, and assurance is part of the doctrine of sanctification. Therefore we shall first examine assurance, as explained by Bishop Ryle; and after that we shall try to complete this part of the subject by an examination of perseverance.

Bishop J.C. Ryle, a most devout Christian, wrote a now well-known book on _Holiness_ (reprinted by Kregel, 1952). Its second chapter has the title "Sanctification." He defends the importance of the doctrine by saying, "Unless we are sanctified, we shall not be saved" (p. 15). The Catechism defines "Sanctification [as] the work of God's free grace, whereby we are renewed in the whole man after the image of God, and are enabled more and more to die to sin and live unto righteousness." Bishop Ryle says much the same thing: "Sanctification is that inward spiritual work which the Lord Jesus Christ works in a man by the Holy Ghost, when he calls him to be a true believer. He not only washes him from his sins in his own blood, but he also _separates_ him from his natural love of sin and the world, puts a new principle in his heart, and makes him practically godly in life. The instrument by which the Spirit effects this work is generally the Word of God."

Here Bishop Ryle has gone beyond the *definition* of sanctification, as neither the Shorter nor the Larger Catechism does, and adds a statement of the method by which sanctification can be carried on. It is the study of the Word. The present treatise very strongly recommends Bible study, very strongly indeed.

Bishop Ryle, however, seems to allow an exception: "generally the Word of God, though he [the Spirit] sometimes uses afflictions and providential visitations 'without the word' (I Peter 3:1)." That God may use afflictions for this purpose can hardly be doubted; but one may doubt that sanctification can ever proceed without the Word. The verse Ryle uses does not really support his wording. Peter pictures a Christian wife of a pagan husband. She has already given him the Word, and he remains stubbornly disobedient to it. Thus the man already knows the gospel, and it annoys him. Repetition would only irritate him further. Therefore Peter advises the wife to cease her preaching the Word and to win him by her pious *behavior* (the King James term *conversation* is an antiquated usage). But it should be obvious to all that no man can be won to Christ without having heard the gospel. Furthermore, Ryle is supposedly speaking of sanctification. Peter refers to regeneration. If then Ryle's interpretation of Peter were true, a man could be regenerated without the Word and faith would not come by hearing. But no one is regenerated without the gospel except those very few and exceptional cases who, like John the Baptist, were regenerated in their mother's womb. It is even more impossible to be sanctified without the Scriptures, for only the Word instructs us in the methods to be used.

If anyone object to these remarks as carping criticism of a godly man, Bishop Ryle himself justifies them. "The subject before us is of such deep and vast importance that it requires fencing, guarding, clearing up, and marking out on every side. A doctrine which is needful to salvation can never be too sharply developed or brought too fully to light." And he continues in this vein for several more lines. If Ryle thought such exactitude a desideratum in the nineteenth century, how much more is it necessary in this sloppy, anti-doctrinal, anti-intellectual twentieth century! The present age has modified a line of poetry and acts on the principle, "Ignorance is bliss, 'tis folly to be wise." A certain Presbytery in 1981 licensed a seminary graduate after an examination in which he was not able to answer a single question put to him. Unfortunately I was the only presbyter who asked him a question. Well, maybe, fortunately. Sanctification depends on a knowledge of the Word, and God's word is worthy of "fencing, guarding, clearing up, and marking out on every side."

This emphasis on Bible study and doctrine can never be too great and hardly ever too much repeated. Toward the end of his book Ryle (with more devotion to the Church of England than I like) produces a monumental paragraph, needed today much more than then.

> The men who have done most for the Church of England, and made the deepest mark on their day and generation, have always been men of most decided and distinct doctrinal views. It is the bold, decided, outspoken man, like Capel Nolyneux, or our grand old Protestant champion Hugh McNeile, who makes a great impression, and sets people thinking, and "turns the world up-side down." It was "dogma" in the apostolic ages which emptied the heathen temples and shook Greece and Rome. It was "dogma" which awoke Christendom from its slumbers at the time of the Reformation and spoiled the Pope of one third of his subjects. It was "dogma" which 100 years ago revived the Church of England in the days of White-field, Wesley, Venn, and Romaine, and blew up our

dying Christianity into a burning flame. . . . Let us cling to decided doctrinal views, whatever some may please to say in these times, and we shall do well for ourselves, well for others, well for the Church of England, and well for Christ's cause in the world (p. 298).

Omit the name of Wesley and reduce the Church of England to one reference, and the whole could have come down *senkrecht vom oben.*

Realizing, in opposition to Wesley, that Romans 7 describes Christian struggles and not an unregenerate lack of struggle, Ryle comforts Christians by pointing out that the struggle is itself an evidence of sanctification rather than an evidence of its lack (p. 21). He explicitly rejects "sinless perfection." His interests lead him to picture what seems to have been a common phenomenon of religion in England, but one that can hardly be found in America today. His aim is to show what sanctification is not. The first point is:

> True sanctification then does not consist in *talk about religion.* This . . . ought never to be forgotten [note the emphasis]. The vast increase of education in these latter days makes it absolutely necessary to raise a warning voice. People hear so much of Gospel truth that they contract an unholy familiarity with its words and phrases and sometimes talk so fluently about its doctrines that you might think them true Christians (p. 24).

Today in America public education has so silenced the teaching of the Bible, while utilizing pornographic textbooks, that about the only Biblical event that most people know is the story of David and Goliath. Some do not know even that. I have had students in the university who told

me they had never read a single line in the Bible at all. They
know all about sex and drugs, but nothing about sanctification. Of course, Ryle is right in denying that sanctification is
"flippant language . . . about 'conversion, the Savior, the
Gospel, finding peace, free grace;' " but today if the term
conversion is sometimes used, the Savior is not mentioned,
and *free grace* conveys no meaning whatever. Would that
there were some hypocrites in this era: It would be
evidence of social improvement.

Ryle continues to show what sanctification is not. It is
not the "animal excitement" produced by wild evangelistic
campaigns. Nor does it consist in the opposite "outward
formalism and external devoutness" (p. 28): "constant
attendance on church services, reception of the Lord's
Supper, and observance of fasts and saints days, in multiplied bowings and turnings . . . and the use of pictures and
crosses." This denial is still pertinent for Romanism and
Anglicanism, but otherwise unimportant today. What may
be more to the point in the case of Pentecostals and
holiness groups today is his denial that sanctification
consists in "retirement from our place in life." Ryle has in
mind "monasteries and convents," but the phrase can
include the less extreme forms such as the Mennonites'
white bonnet. There was also the girl of marriageable age
who, when asked politely, not superciliously, by a secular
gentleman, what were the tenets of her religion, answered,
"Well, in the first place, we do not wear lipstick." The
gentleman made no reply to her, but later he told others he
could not be interested in what came in second place. No
doubt a Christian woman should be modest, but modesty
in ancient Rome was more a matter of avoiding elaborate,
jeweled hairdos than bikinis.

Turning from what sanctification is not, Ryle says
positively, "Genuine sanctification will show itself in *habitual respect to God's law,*" and what is the same thing,

"Genuine sanctification will show itself in an *habitual* endeavor to do Christ's will" (p. 27). In fact he repeats the same idea in five paragraphs. Once more this enforces the necessity of the major requirement for advancing in sanctification, *viz.*, Bible study. The distinction between divine requirements and silly superstitions can be maintained only by a careful exegesis of Scripture.

There is one point at which I believe Ryle and others to be confused or at least careless. After quoting "There is a time to weep and a time to laugh," Ryle declares "but there is no time, no, not a day, in which a man ought not to be holy. Are we?" This confuses two senses of the term *holy*. The Old Testament refers to things and persons as holy in being set apart for the Lord's service. The instruments in the Tabernacle were holy; and the priests were holy, though not always sanctified. This type of holiness is not what is meant by the verse which says, "Without holiness no man shall see the Lord." It is not true that only priests shall see the Lord. Even the verse itself, apart from priests, and if detached from the rest of Scripture, can give a false impression. The point is that there are degrees of holiness and sanctification. In an absolute sense, the question, "Are we" holy, can be answered only in the negative. One should ask, Am I increasing in holiness? Ryle of course is well aware of all this, but authors, like the present also, slip into inexactitudes which can confuse careless readers. Ryle continues, "A man may go to great lengths and yet never reach true holiness" (p. 34). This form of expression seems to present holiness as a seamless robe, an all or nothing. Of course Ryle adds, "A holy man will *endeavor* to shun every *known* sin." He "will *strive* to be like our Lord. . . . A holy man will *follow after* meekness . . . temperance . . . purity of heart . . ." (pp. 36, 37). Then he says explicitly, "Sanctification is always a progressive work" (p. 39). Perhaps I am overly critical of his previous inadequate phrases; but if so, it is because I have had contacts with alleged sinless perfectionists and some contemporary Pentecostalists.

The perfectionist groups, Wesleyans and Pentecostals, seem to have the idea that after a struggle or two, a Christian, a true Christian, who has the "full gospel," arrives at a state of perfect peace and victory. Foreign to their thought is the hymn

> Must I be carried to the skies,
> On flowery beds of ease,
> When others fought to win the prize,
> And sailed through bloody seas?

To counteract such ideas Ryle's fourth chapter warns the readers of "The Fight." In addition to the holiness groups who think they have already attained, there are others who avoid fighting only because they are not inclined to do so. The former have ostensibly stopped fighting; the latter and much more numerous group has never begun.

Ryle quotes several pertinent verses: "Fight the good fight," "mortify your members which are upon the earth," and Romans 7:23, 24. The difficulty in writing a "how to" book lies in the fact that the situations, the temptations, and weaknesses of individual Christians are so various that what applies concretely to one Christian is of no interest to another. Once I was faintly acquainted with a minister who had a drinking problem, on Saturday nights, too! But a hundred others are not so tempted, not in the least. I have been better acquainted with at least four ministers who committed adultery. But I hope a thousand others have not. One minister, whom I knew slightly, during the great depression of the 1930's resorted to theft to feed his family. The Presbytery, in striking his name from the roll, was nonetheless very sympathetic.

Hence when Ryle says that the Christian soldier must fight the flesh, must fight the world, must fight the devil (pp. 52, 53), he speaks the truth, but says nothing very helpful. Perhaps a personal counselor could be helpful, for he would be acquainted with the individual's needs. Ryle's scriptural quotations, of course, and his exhortations are good, and each Christian can apply them to himself. But the most important of all, because indubitably fundamental, is the exhortation to study the Scripture: "A religion without doctrine or dogma is a thing which many are fond of talking of in the present day." And many, many more in this ecumenical, neo-orthodox, existential century. But "No man will ever be anything or do anything in religion, unless he believes *something*" (p. 57). Ryle then very properly urges a belief or faith "in our Lord Jesus Christ's person, work, and office." You and I then must apply the principles to our individual problems.

Nearly everybody, well, every serious and honest person, would profit from reading Ryle. But since there is so much repetition, it would seem better to read a page a day for ten days rather than a hundred pages at one sitting.

One subhead under the general title of Sanctification or Holiness is Assurance. Calvin and the first generation of Reformers seem to have held that assurance is inseparable from faith. Whoever is not assured of his salvation is simply not saved. This view may have been encouraged by the severity of Romish persecution, the exuberance of a newly found faith, and the utter impossibility of finding assurance in penance and good works. But as the persecutions diminished and as calmer study could be undertaken, the Westminster divines, a full century later, wrote, "This infallible assurance doth not so belong to the essence of faith, but that a true believer may wait long, and conflict with many difficulties, before he is partaker of it" (XVIII, 3).

I must confess I do not like the word *infallible* in this

context. The Pope claims infallibility, but if this is a false claim, it seems strange that it can be asserted of a thousand or a million Protestants. One of the older divines, whose name I have forgotten, illustrated infallibility by the knowledge of a ship captain's guiding his ship into a harbor. Though the captain was ignorant of many things, and mistaken about many others, he *infallibly* knew the channel. But is it not possible, as it actually happened in 1983 when a naval vessel struck a sand bar in San Francisco Bay, that a storm could have closed the previous channel? Scripture is infallible; nothing else is. We all can and we all do make mistakes.

Ryle does not seem to realize this. Nor do many others. Those who are so assured about assurance do not seem to understand the difficulties. Once I had a very friendly conversation with a college professor who was strongly Arminian. I remarked that one difference between Calvinism and Arminianism was that the latter denied the possibility of assurance. "Not so," he replied, "I'm right now completely assured of my salvation. If I should die this moment, I know I would go to heaven. Of course," he continued, "if I should live until tomorrow or next week, I do not know whether I shall be saved or not." This raises the question of the value of assurance. Assurance of salvation does not mean that you will get to heaven. Assurance that a good restaurant serves good food does not guarantee that it serves good food. My major professor in graduate school took his wife out one Saturday night to a restaurant which he had often patronized. Before the night was over, he had died of food poisoning. His assurance had been misplaced. Many people are assured of all sorts of things. Some are sure that drinking vinegar will cure warts. But assurance guarantees nothing.

Like so many other authors, Ryle does not face the difficulties squarely. He begins by noting Paul's assurance and confidence expressed in II Timothy 4:6, 7, 8. "The Apostle speaks without any hesitation or distrust" (p. 101). There can be no quarrel with Ryle's four main points: (1) Paul's assurance was Scriptural; (2) a man may have no assurance and yet be saved; (3) assurance is desirable; and (4) assurance is seldom attained. No quarrel? It seems to me that millions of people, even many who do not profess to be Christians, are sure of arriving in heaven. Quite commonly it is said that God is too good to punish anyone. Maybe Ryle's words correctly described the conditions in England a century ago, but it is doubtful that it is true in America today.

Having the opinion that assurance is rare, Ryle extends its possibility to every Christian (p. 103). He allows that Rome denies this possibility. True. And also, "the vast majority of the worldly and thoughtless Christians among ourselves oppose the doctrine." Possibly true then, but very likely false now. However, Job 19:25-27, Psalm 23:4, 6, Isaiah 26:3, and 32:17, Romans 8:39 on to I John 5:19 insist that assurance is possible. Not only was assurance possible in apostolic times, but "many have attained to such an assured hope ... even in modern times" (p. 105). This certainly seems to be what the Bible teaches; but Ryle, at least so far, has not told us how to attain such assurance and how to distinguish it from careless presumption or from what Louis Berkhof calls "temporary faith," so little temporary as to last a lifetime.

On the second point Ryle clearly asserts that some true "believers never arrive at this assured hope" (p. 107). His third point, that "an assured hope is exceedingly to be desired," hardly needs any discussion at all. He spends seven pages on it.

His fourth point is "some probable causes why an assured hope is so seldom attained." He lists "a defective view of the doctrine of justification." But this is far from showing that a correct understanding of justification must result in an infallible assurance. The same reply is applicable also to the second reason: "slothfulness about growth in grace." It is likely that the contraries of these deficiencies are *necessary* for assurance, but there is no evidence that they are *sufficient*. This makes the argument irrelevant. His third reason only repeats the second. And that is the end of the argument. The final three pages of the chapter are excellent exhortations to holiness, but they propose no sure method for attaining infallible surety.

Perhaps someone will say that it is wrong to seek for a method of achieving assurance. It is a gift of God, we cannot earn it, there is nothing for us to do except to hope that God favors us. Well, it is true that assurance, like faith, is a gift of God, but though regeneration and faith can have no preparation on our part, assurance or at least sanctification requires certain actions by us. Perhaps *method* is not the proper term, but John tells us that "These things have I written to you that believe on the name of the Son of God, that ye may have eternal life." The usual exegesis of "these things" that John wrote is that faith, love, and obedience, while they do not automatically produce assurance, are none the less requirements for being a candidate, so to speak, to receive it. Actually love is one form of obedience, since it is commanded, and hence belief and overt obedience are the two prerequisites.

There is, however, a difficulty. It is the same one Luther struggled with before he discovered the doctrine of justification. In Romanism he was supposed to earn his salvation by good works, penance, flagellation, and various monkish practices. But, being very sincere, he was troubled because he could never be sure that he had done enough. A similar difficulty arises here. If we wish to distinguish a valid assurance from a false assurance, how can we know that we have a sufficient theological knowledge and a sufficient degree of obedience to have met the requirements? Do we love deeply enough? Have we satisfied John's criteria? Is there any devotional writer who has forthrightly faced this problem? It is hard to believe that none of them has thought of it. If, as previously stated, Louis Berkhof's temporary faith can last a lifetime, how can the true be identified in contrast with the false?

4. Perseverance

As a partial answer to the perplexities of assurance, as an unmasking of the Wesleyan divergence from Scripture, and as a further step in developing the subject of sanctification, perseverance, the fifth of the five points of the Calvinistic TULIP, compels attention.

In opposition to the Arminian doctrine that a man may be regenerate at breakfast, lost at lunch, and re-regenerated at dinner, or what is much worse, never regenerated again and finally lost, the Westminster Confession says, "Those whom God hath accepted in the Beloved, effectually called and sanctified by his Spirit, can neither totally nor finally fall away from the state of grace, but shall certainly persevere therein to the end and be eternally saved" (XVII, 1; compare 2 and 3). This doctrine is so frequently and forcefully stated, in both the Old and New Testaments, that it is hard to explain how any Christian can be an Arminian.

To begin with, Job 17:9 says, "The righteous shall hold to his way, and he who has clean hands shall grow stronger and stronger." This verse in the book of Job is a statement by Job himself, and not one by his false friends who, though they may have spoken the truth at times, are condemned toward the end of the book. Hence we may trust it as true, rather than question it as possibly an evil pronouncement.

The verse rather clearly, indeed unmistakably, indicates that a regenerate sinner will persevere. Though he may stumble and fall, though he may be temporarily overcome by weakness, he shall hold to his way; and not only so, but also he will grow stronger and stronger.

Next is Psalm 84:5-7, "Blessed is the man whose strength is in thee: in whose heart are the ways of them. . . . They go from strength to strength, every one of them in Zion appeareth before God." These verses also are pellucid. There is no hint of any falling away. See also Psalm 94:14, "The Lord will not cast off his people, neither will he forsake his inheritance." Then comes Psalm 125:1-2, "They that trust in the Lord shall be as Mount Zion, which cannot be removed, but abideth forever. As the mountains are round about Jerusalem, so the Lord is round about his people from henceforth even forever." Establishing the doctrine of perseverance is furthered by referring to its basis in the eternal decree and in the immutability of God, as the last two verses indicate. The very nature of God, as described in the Bible, guarantees perseverance. Arminianism simply does not have the Biblical concept of God.

Then too, the words of Isaiah 40:28-31 should be ineradicably engraved on every Christian's memory: "Hast thou not known . . . the everlasting God . . . fainteth not neither is weary. . . . He giveth power to the faint and . . . increaseth strength. . . . they that wait upon the Lord shall renew their strength . . . shall run and not be weary, they shall walk and not faint."

With a great effort it is just possible to imagine an Arminian reply to these verses. Does not Psalm 125 refer to those "who trust in the Lord"? If they cease trusting, they will not abide forever. Similarly Isaiah speaks of those "that will wait upon the Lord:" and naturally if they get tired of waiting, they will not appear before God in Zion. This Arminian exegesis might achieve plausibility if other verses were missing such as Psalm 24:5-7, already quoted, and several others yet to be quoted. However, the two verses in dispute, Psalm 125:1-2 and Isaiah 40:28-31, are not so easily fitted into an Arminian interpretation. The former speaks of "his people." Not only cannot they be removed, but also the Lord is round about them forever. If the Lord is round about Joe Doaks of Speedunk today, he will be round about him forever, and Joe D. can never be lost. Similarly Isaiah 40:28-31 indicates that there are Christians, to whom the Lord will give power and strength. If they are now waiting upon the Lord, the Lord will cause them to mount up with wings as eagles. Nor do these words apply to some Christians only. The promise is without exception.

We now pass on to Jeremiah 32:40. "And I will make an everlasting covenant with them, that I will not turn away from them, to do them good; but I will put my fear in their hearts, that they shall not depart from me." Observe carefully that the covenant is everlasting, not temporary. God will not cease to do them good. He will instill permanent devotion in their hearts, so that "they shall not turn away from me." This is another refutation of the perverse exegesis alluded to a paragraph or two ago. Notice that God will, and they shall. The fruition of the everlasting covenant depends on God's decree and power, and because of this they shall never turn away.

Since the Calvinist accuses the Arminian of proving too much by his interpretations, so the Arminian might say that the Calvinistic Jeremiah promises too much. Do not Christians turn away? Do they not sin? And does not the Calvinistic interpretation contradict the evident facts? All Christians, except a few, and these only late in life, are imperfect. We agree, except for the exception. Calvinists admit and insist that all, even those near death, continue to sin. But if the words of Jeremiah are given an Arminian interpretation, favorable to sinless perfection, a conclusion follows that no Arminian can accept, *viz.*, it is not just a few people at death's door who become sinless, but every Christian from the moment of conversion on. This was said before in connection with I John 3:9, and it applies here as well, for there is no exception to the *they* and the *them* in Jeremiah 32:40; nor is the "not depart" limited to a short time before one's death.

Perseverance does not mean uninterrupted progress at the same or an ever increasing rate. In ordinary affairs we speak of a man persevering who falls, blunders, receives set-backs, but who recovers and struggles on. This is why Calvinists use and prefer the term *perseverance* rather than the Arminian deceptive phrase "eternal security." The latter in itself gives no hint of struggle; the former does.

If the Old Testament is so clear on this matter, it is really not necessary to quote the New Testament also. But as such an omission would surely be misunderstood by the Arminians, and since in any case we wish to know what the New Testament says, here are some verses.

John 10:28, 29: "And I give unto them eternal life; and they shall never perish, neither shall any man pluck them out of my hand. My Father, which gave them me, is greater than all; and no man is able to pluck them out of my Father's hand."

It must be a most elementary student and immature Christian who is unfamiliar with John 10:28-29. And it must be a most confused mentality that cannot understand it correctly. "They shall never perish." Could anything be easier or plainer? Who are the "they"? They are Christ's sheep; Christ knows them all by name; he gives them eternal life, a life that is everlasting. Clearly a life that lasts only a year or two is not eternal. "They shall never perish" is written with a double negative, and double negatives in Greek do not make an affirmative, but an emphatic negative. As if that were not enough Christ adds, "Neither shall any man pluck them out of my hand." Relative to this phrase I either read or heard an Arminian say that although no man can pluck a Christian out of God's hand, the word *man* means "no other man;" but the man himself can pluck himself out of God's hand. I have no documentation for this, and it may not be typical of all Wesleyans. But at any rate, the word in the New Testament is *tis*, anyone, including the man himself as well as Satan. Then to pile emphasis upon emphasis Jesus continues, "My Father is greater than all, and no one is able to pluck them out of my Father's hand."

To escape such utterly unambiguous verses the Arminians are forced to invent utterly ridiculous misinterpretations, for otherwise they would have to repudiate their beloved free will and become Calvinists—a disaster not to be contemplated.

If these numerous quotations begin to bore the reader —and well they may because they all say the same thing with utter clarity—nonetheless let the reader submit to still more boredom. It makes the doctrine of perseverance painfully clear. Therefore supererogatorially we quote Romans 11:29, for Paul is no less clear than Jesus was. The verse may be translated "the gift and calling of God are irrevocable" (New American Standard). Next comes I Corinthians 1:8, ". . . our Lord Jesus Christ, who shall confirm you to the end, blameless in the day of our Lord Jesus Christ." If the Arminians say that the verse teaches sinless perfection, they must accept the conclusion that all Christians will become sinless, not just some of the more superannuated. Well, all Christians will indeed become sinless at the day of our Lord Jesus Christ; but the Arminians have in mind only a very few, and these became sinless (some of them) a thousand years before the day of Christ. This is not what I Corinthians 1:8 means. Philippians 1:6 is equally explicit, even more so, for it says that God, if ever he begins a good work, will perfect it until the day of Christ. This is utterly inconsistent with the Arminian view that God fails to continue his goodness and that a regenerate Christian can finally be lost. Paul expands the sense of the verse in 2:13. He exhorts us to work out our own salvation in fear and trembling. What a fine Arminian sentiment! We must work out our own salvation! But this is not the end of the sentence; Paul continues, "for it is God who works in you, both to will and to do, of his good pleasure." The Arminian theory of free will allows the most devout Christian to nullify God's plan by a rebellious will that God cannot control. But this verse teaches that not only does God control our external works, but also that he controls our very volitions. Whatever God's pleasure is for our will, that we will. Now, it is God's pleasure to complete and perfect the work he began in his elect. Therefore the elect shall never perish and no one can bring them to ruin, neither Satan, nor the individual himself.

Peter agrees with Paul. In his first epistle (1:5) he says, "God . . . hath begotten us . . . to an inheritance incorruptible . . . reserved for you, who are kept by the power of God, through faith unto salvation ready to be revealed in the last time." The first line of this quotation affirms that the inheritance is incorruptible; toward the end the heirs are in view. These heirs of salvation are kept by the power of God, until their salvation is complete at the last day. In the beginning God chose a people for salvation. These people the Father gave to Christ. Since God is immutable, he cannot relinquish his people and purpose; therefore either he lacks power and his purpose fails, or he is omnipotent and succeeds.

To bring to an end such an interminable list of verses, we shall return to Isaiah 14:24, 27. "The Lord of hosts has sworn, saying, 'Surely just as I have intended, so it has happened, and just as I have planned, so it will stand. . . .

For the Lord of Hosts has planned, and who can frustrate [it, or him]? His hand is stretched out and who will turn it back?" Verse 24 is immediately directed against the Assyrians; but the reason is not that the Assyrians are weak. The argument is that God is omnipotent, and therefore one can be sure he will defeat the Assyrians because none of his purposes can fail. The Arminians must deny that God is omnipotent, assert that he changes his mind, or that he did not purpose to save anyone in particular. They must also deny omniscience, for if he really knew that Peter would be saved and that Judas would be lost, free will could never alter their destinies. Omniscience allows no alternate possibilities.

To conclude this subhead on perseverance, it is well to note—though the idea can hardly have been missed through the discussion—that perseverance is inseparately conjoined with the eternal decree, unconditional election, and the covenant of grace. Each is supported severally by various Scriptural passages, but logically they form an indestructible, systematic whole. Any other theory of sanctification is simply not Christianity.

5. The Sacraments

To many readers it may seem strange that a discussion of the sacraments should occur in an exposition of sanctification. Does not sanctification, negatively, have to do with resisting temptation to drunkenness, with breaking the habit of lying, with controlling anger and the tendency to malicious gossip? And positively with practicing patience, hope, aiding the poor, and having a quiet time every morning? John Bunyan's description of the Christian life in *Pilgrim's Progress* has no sacraments in it. If indeed the sacraments merit a discussion, should it not come under the heading of ecclesiology, or be given a division of its own? How can baptism and the Lord's Supper be a means of grace and advance one's degree of sanctification? Or, even if the Lord's Supper, bringing to mind the death of Christ, has some sanctifying effect, how can baptism and particularly infant baptism be productive of Christian achievement? No doubt the sacraments are commanded, and the church should adminster them; but can they be means of grace by which sin is conquered and holiness advanced? Yet Charles Hodge put "The Sacraments" in chapter XX, under the title "The Means of Grace."

Something can indeed be said even for the rite of baptism. At the very least, when a baptized person witnesses the baptism of another in a church service and sees the sign of the divine promises, he is reminded of those promises; and similarly to being assured by the rainbow today that God's promise to Noah is still good, he will be strengthened in his faith. But there is more, at the very least more emphasis, in the New Testament. It seems to me that superstitious sacramentalism has its opposite extreme in the carelessness and lack of reverence found both in some of the evangelistic independent churches and also in the socialistic leftwing denominations. A sincere Christian should try to be entirely Scriptural. The apostle Paul frequently exhorts the Christians to consider their baptism, and he appeals to it in connection with their sanctification. Romans 6 is addressed to those who had been baptized sometime in the past: "Know ye not that so many of us as were baptized into Jesus Christ were baptized into his death?" (Romans 6:3, 4).

Therefore [!] we ought to live a life of sanctification and struggle against sin. This chapter, where Paul refutes the antinomian charges against justification by faith, makes emphatic use of the significance of baptism. Note Romans 6:6: "Knowing this, that our old man was crucified with him [in the baptism into Christ's death] that—in order that —the body of sin might be destroyed. . . ."

Further Paul's appeals to baptism as significant for sanctification are found in Galatians 3:27 and Colossians 2:11, both of which should be understood in the context of their respective chapters.

If now this is sufficient to indicate some connection between the sacraments and sanctification, it is requisite to study the nature of a sacrament as such, *i.e.,* the characteristics common to both sacraments, and then the special characteristics of each one. The questions that arise with respect to the sacraments as such include (1) the definition of a sacrament, (2) the identification or number of sacraments, and (3) their force, value, or significance. Without this knowledge sanctification will be retarded.

The answer to the first of these questions also determines the answer to the second. What is a sacrament? The Shorter Catechism replies, "A sacrament is a holy ordinance instituted by Christ; wherein, by sensible signs, Christ and the benefits of the new covenant are represented, sealed, and applied to believers."

Romanism holds that there are seven sacraments: baptism, confirmation, the eucharist, penance, extreme unction, order, and matrimony. Although the Council of Trent insists that all of these were instituted by Jesus Christ our Lord, extreme unction and matrimony seem to have no such basis. Extreme unction has no biblical basis at all, and matrimony, certainly ordained of God, is not restricted to Christians. Order or ordination is a New Testament procedure, for I Timothy refers to bishops and deacons, and in 4:14 speaks of ordination by the presbytery. The ministry, however, is not a sensible sign representing something it is literally not. Water is. If confirmation is the reception into the congregation of a new communicant member, it too is not a sign; nor does there seem to be in the New Testament any rite of reception other than baptism. Penance, as practiced by Romanism, might be a sensible sign, but it is regularly regarded as the actual suffering of a penalty. At any rate, *repentance* as taught in Scripture, is not a sign, but a literal reality. Therefore the only *sensible signs, representing the benefits of the new covenant,* and *instituted by Christ,* are the signs of baptism and the Lord's Supper.

The more important point, however, is the significance and efficacy of the sacraments. Although Canon VII of the seventh session of Trent (March 3, 1547) speaks of receiving the sacraments *rightly—etiam si rite ea suscipiant—*the adverb *rite* merely means "according to the customary usage." Thus in the next canon there occurs the phrase that Protestants have always condemned: *"ex opere operato."* The canon reads, "If anyone saith that by the said sacraments of the New Law grace is not conferred *through the act performed,* but that faith alone in the divine promise suffices for the obtaining of grace: let him be anathema." And the next canon speaks of baptism, confirmation, and order as "imprinting in the soul a character, that is, a certain spiritual and indelible sign, . . ." To insure that imprinting, the only internal disposition, as differentiated from simply "going through the motions," *ex opere operato,* is the intention of the priest to do what the church does (Canon XI). As Attwater's *Catholic Dictionary* says, "Sacrament: A sacred sensible sign . . . to confer that [sanctifying] grace on the soul of the recipient. A sacrament is not fulfilled *by the fact that one believes in it* [Protestant italics] but by the fact that it is made. . . . Sacraments cause grace. . . ."

Note here that a recipient's belief in the sacrament does not make it efficacious. It takes effect "by the fact that it is made"—*ex opere operato.* Whether the recipient believes or does not believe seems immaterial. Romanists admit, we grant, that if the recipient imposes some obstacle in the ceremony, the sacrament has no effect. But such an obstacle is not so much ignorance or a lack of faith as it is a deliberate rejection of the sacrament's function. The sacrament works, *ex opere operato,* in infants, in the ignorant, and even in pagans who carelessly or with a shrug of the shoulders permit a priest to go through the motions. The recipient need not believe in the efficacy of the sacrament. Only the priest need believe, or at least intend to do what the church says.

The *New Catholic Encyclopedia* apparently tries to avoid the opprobrium of such a doctrine and uses language that seems to require faith in the recipient. But, first, this hardly agrees with the official position of the Roman church that the sacrament works *ex opere operato.* And in the second place the words of the *Encyclopedia* may require nothing more than implicit faith, which is no better than ignorance and may comport with undiscovered heresy.

Protestants sometimes refer to this view as reducing the sacraments to the level of magic; and one can also observe priests mumbling some Latin phrases over crucifixes and other pieces of jewelry. The force of this distaste for Romish ceremonies, however, does not lie precisely in the word *magic:* but rather the more profound and Biblical position that God does not use magic. Magic formulas are supposed to work automatically, *ex opere operato,* regardless of belief in them. But the Scriptures show that God requires knowledge, understanding, faith, and sincerity on the part of the worshipper. Repentance is a change of mind, not the act of wearing a hair shirt; and it is a change of mind, not on the part of a priest, but on the part of the convert. Repentance, participating in a sacrament, like prayer—prayer that God will receive—demands sincerity and obedience. In the prophecy of Isaiah God issues appalling denunciations against the Israelites in their no doubt meticulous ritualism. Not only were their *sacrifices* abominations, but God also refused to hear their *prayers.* Jesus, too, in Matthew 15:8 quotes Isaiah 29 and says, "Hypocrites! Well did Isaiah prophesy of you saying, This people draweth nigh unto me with their mouth, and honoreth me with their lips, but their heart is far from me." Does this really mean that if the priest had good intentions, it made no difference whether or not the people believed in it?

In opposition to the Romish position that a sacrament conveys grace to a recipient even though he does not believe in it, the following data are applicable:

> Acts 2:41: Then they that gladly received his word were baptized.
>
> Acts 10:47: Can any man forbid water, that these should not be baptized, which have received the Holy Ghost as well as we?
>
> Romans 4:11: And he received the sign of circumcision, a seal of the righteousness of the faith which he had yet being uncircumcised: that he might be the father of all them that believe, though they be not circumcised: that righteousness might be imputed unto them also. . . .

The force of the two verses in Acts does not lie in any explicit assertion that the recipient must be a believer. They state that the recipients in question were as a matter of fact believers. Their force, however, depends on the absence, throughout Scripture, of any commendatory examples of unbelieving recipients. In the case of infant baptism the parents must have faith; but this apparent exception, which Baptists will no doubt emphasize, is to be considered below under baptism. The other sacraments, however, are administered to adults: eucharist, penance, order, matrimony, confirmation, extreme unction. Now, it seems peculiar that the sacrament of order, the ordination of a priest, is effective even though the ordinand does not believe in it. The result is that an unbelieving priest can then administer these rites with effect, if only, while he does not believe in them, he still intends to do what the church intends.

But back to the last list of verses. More positive than the first two is Romans 4:11. The sacrament is there described as the seal of the faith which the recipient had before he received the sacrament. This passage is not to be taken simply as one instance among many, as the verses in Acts were. On the contrary, this passage describes the institution and purpose of the sacrament. If circumcision was instituted as a sign of the faith Abraham already had, then the Romanists have no grounds for asserting that in other instances the recipient need not be a believer. The same point is emphasized in Romans 2:25-29: "Circumcision verily profiteth, if thou keep the law; but . . . . For he is not a Jew which is one outwardly . . . , but he is a Jew, which is one inwardly . . . of the heart, in the spirit. . . ."

Unrighteousness nullifies the rite. The outward motions or the outward profession is useless. He is a believer who is one inwardly. The situation described in these verses allows the priest to be pious and sincere. He may have the strongest intentions to do what the church does. But if the recipient is an unbeliever, the priest's ministrations are useless. It is not the performance of the ritual, nor the intention of the priest, but the belief of the recipient that makes the sacrament.

Consider the following as well:

> I Corinthians 11:27-29: Wherefore whosoever shall eat this bread, and drink this cup of the Lord, unworthily, shall be guilty of the body and blood of the Lord. But let a man examine himself, and so let him eat of that bread, and drink of that cup. For he that eateth and drinketh unworthily, eateth and and drinketh damnation to himself, not discerning the Lord's body.

> I Peter 3:21: The like figure whereunto even
> baptism doth also now save us (not the putting away
> of the filth of the flesh, but the answer of a good
> conscience toward God), by the resurrection of Jesus
> Christ.

The first of the above two passages is utterly conclusive against Romanism. It states that a person may partake of the Lord's Supper and instead of receiving grace will receive condemnation, as being guilty of the body and blood of the Lord. In such a case the sacrament is not effective *ex opere operato*. With this warning the Apostle commands the prospective recipient to examine himself. The individual must assure himself that he believes, and only so should he receive the elements. And then verse 29 repeats the sentence of damnation on unbelievers, or a sentence of sickness and physical death on careless believers. This is decisive and incontrovertible. The verse in I Peter corroborates the preceding by insisting on a good conscience—regardless of how other phrases in the verse are exegeted. But since I Peter is not so detailed and explicit, nothing further than corroboration need be made of it.

If it now be agreed that the recipient must have faith, even if in an unusual and regrettable case the minister does not, Protestants are willing to say that the sacraments are effective means of grace. But the grace and the effect are not what Rome says they are.

It is therefore requisite to make a few more remarks on the efficacy of sacraments. Baptism and the Lord's Supper are ceremonies commanded by Christ. Therefore the church must administer them until Christ returns. They are signs: Baptism signifies purification, and the Supper pictures Christ's death. The sacraments are also seals which confirm our faith, and as such are means of grace. A seal, in earlier legal practice, showed that a document was genuine. If seals are no longer so widely used, at least they were familiar necessities in Biblical times (compare I Kings 21:8, Nehemiah 9:38, Isaiah 8:16, Jeremiah 32:10, Daniel 12:4). In the case of Abraham and his descendants, circumcision was the seal God placed on his promises. One might argue that God and God's promises do not need seals: nevertheless God used seals to strengthen our assurance.

However, if God has made no promises, if the document is blank, if there is nothing to seal, the seal obviously is useless. Hence with the seal there must also be the Scripture whose truth is thereby authenticated. Sacraments are not to be celebrated apart from the Word.

A magical formula operates of itself; it needs nothing further. Hence Romish worship most frequently has its sacraments without the Word, whereas Calvinism always stresses the sermon—the preaching of the Word. Without the Word the sacrament seals nothing. For a sacrament to be effective, it must be understood; and the more extensive the understanding the greater the effect. Suppose Nebuchadnezzar had sent a sealed document to the Chinese. Unless the Chinese had a translator, the document would mean nothing to them. This is why the Protestants from the first insisted on translating the Bible into the common languages, while the Roman church, until only a few years ago, opposed translations for the people. Incidentally, this is also why Paul insists that the miraculous gift of speaking in foreign languages, during the apostolic age, should not be used in public unless translation were also given. Thus "There is never any sacrament," says Calvin (*Institutes* IV xiv 3, 4), "without an antecedent promise of God, to which it is subjoined as an appendix. . . . A sacrament consists of the Word and the outward sign. For we ought to understand the *word,* not of a murmur uttered without any meaning or faith, a mere whisper like a magical incantation . . . but of the gospel preached. . . ."

While far from exhaustive, this is perhaps enough on the sacraments as such. Some omissions will be filled in as each sacrament is discussed separately.

Baptism

Virtually all churches that claim to be Christian administer the rite of baptism. Exceptions are the Salvation Army and the Quakers. Such groups are guilty of disobeying God's command, for the command to baptize and the command to teach the gospel occur in the same verse: Matthew 28:19: "Teach all nations, baptizing them . . . ." Acts 2:38: "Repent and be baptized."

The solemnity of the sacrament, and the necessity that the church should administer baptism—though baptism is not absolutely necessary for the salvation of a given individual—can be seen in the formula Christ imposed: ". . . baptizing them in the name of the Father, and of the Son, and of the Holy Ghost."

This formula should always be used. The minister may say "I baptize thee . . . ," or, "Robert, child of the covenant, I baptize thee . . . ." or even, "This servant is now baptized . . . ," but always it must be "in the name of the Father, and of the Son, and of the Holy Ghost." But the formula itself is not enough. The recipient must have believed and must have repented, if he is an adult. The minister ought also to believe in the sacrament. If a false minister is pastor of a truly Christian congregation—and this has frequently and unfortunately been the case in the twentieth century—his administration of the rite does not nullify it, for the essential point is the faith of the recipient. But if the rite is performed in and by a heretical or apostate church, then even if the formula is used, it is used only as a mockery, in rejection of God's Word, not only by the minister individually and unknown to the congregation, but officially by the denomination, known publicly. Such a ceremony is not Christian baptism.

Now although nearly all professing churches practice the rite of baptism, they do not all practice it in the same way or with the same intent. The points of difference include (1) by what external means should baptism be administered, (2) who should administer the rite, (3) to whom should it be administered, and (4) with what intent, that is, what is the meaning of the rite and what does it accomplish?

The first of these questions divides in two. Should water alone, or could sand also, be used? The churches that teach baptismal regeneration, to be discussed as point (4), insist that baptism is essential to salvation. Now, it is obvious that the thief on the cross was not baptized with water. For his sake and for the sake of others who may be converted in unusual circumstances—dying of thirst in the middle of the Sahara—the Roman church allows baptism by sand; or if on barren rock or without human companions, baptism "of desire" will do.

There is something strange in this. Canon II on Baptism (March 3, 1547) reads, "If any one say that true and natural water is not of necessity for baptism . . . let him be anathema." Canon V then adds, "If any one saith that baptism is . . . not necessary unto salvation, let him be anathema." But, then, Canon IV on the Sacrament in General (same session) had already said, "If any one saith that the sacraments of the New Law are not necessary unto salvation . . . and that without them, or *without the desire thereof* . . . ." Hence Romanism allows for a baptism without water and without any visible sign or motions. This does not agree with the New Testament. Its examples and its precepts show that water is essential to baptism, but baptism is not essential to heaven.

This leads to the second half of question one: If baptism can be administered only by the application of water, should the water be poured, sprinkled, or should the person be totally immersed? Some such question was raised in the early sub-apostolic church. While it should be maintained that the Scripture alone, and not the immature and confused second century church, settles the question, some instruction can be gained from the *Didachē*. In chapter seven it says, "Baptize . . . in running water, but if thou hast no running water, baptize in other water, and if thou canst not in cold [because the convert is old and infirm?] then in warm. But if thou hast neither [how could the church have neither, and do the following?], pour water three times on the head. . . ." As a testimony to the practices of the early second century, it shows that water was essential, and that it could be applied by pouring. The mention of running water might suggest to some the method of immersion, though this would be an invalid inference; and one also wonders why baptism could not be performed in a lake.

Lutherans and Calvinists do not insist on just one specific method of applying the water. The Lutherans generally pour, as the *Didachē* indicates. The Calvinists generally sprinkle. But both acknowledge that immersion is permissible. The Baptists of course hold that immersion is essential and that sprinkling and pouring are not permissible. One reason the former resist immersion is that too many people think it is necessary, and to accede to their erroneous notions would be to strengthen a wrong idea.

One part of the Baptist defense is that Christ, after being baptized by John, came *out of* the water (Matthew 3:16). The preposition, however, is *apo*, which means *away from*. For example, Acts 3:19 "from the presence of the Lord;" and Acts 5:41, "from the presence of the council," and Acts 7:45, "from before the face of our fathers." Hence this preposition gives no support to immersion: Jesus walked away from the Jordan river. Another Baptist verse would be Acts 8:38-39. Both Philip and the eunuch "went down into the water," and they both "came up out of the water." In this case the people went into and came out of the water—the prepositions are *eis* and *ek*. They surely got their feet wet. But if this meant immersion, Philip would have been immersed as well as the eunuch, for the motions indicated apply to both.

So much for prepositions. Another part of the Baptist argument depends on the verb *baptizo*.

The verb *bapto* occurs only three times in the New Testament, and in none of these is the reference to baptism. The verb means to dip—the end of the finger, a morsel of bread, or a robe. On the other hand *baptizo* occurs about eighty times, plus about twenty-five instances of *baptisma* and *baptismos*. Whether these words are precise synonyms for immersion can be discovered by examining their usage. It is strictly a matter of the Greek language.

The Greek translation of the Old Testament, the Septuagint, made about 200 B.C., in Daniel 4:33 (LXX, 4:30), states that Nebuchadnezzar was baptized with the dew of heaven. He may thus have been very wet, but he certainly was not immersed. While the Apocrypha is not canonical, it is nonetheless a Jewish production in the Greek language, and as such is evidence of what the word meant in those days. Ecclesiasticus 34:25 (LXX 34:30) connects the verb *baptize* with purification. One must wash or baptize oneself after touching a dead body. Numbers 19:13, 20 shows that purification from contact with dead bodies was performed by sprinkling. Hence the verb in the Apocrypha designates sprinkling.

In the New Testament the verb for baptize and another verb for washing are interchangeable. For example, Luke 11:38 uses baptize for washing the hands before meals, while Matthew 15:2, 20 and Mark 7:3 use the other verb for the same thing.

Mark 7:4ff. says that cups, pots, and couches were baptized. It may be that the word *couches* is the insertion of a copyist and should not be regarded as a part of Scripture. But the point here is merely Greek usage. The copyist knew Greek and he wrote that couches were baptized. Now, a cup would very likely be immersed; a brazen vessel would be more difficult to immerse; but it can hardly be credited that couches, on which several people reclined at dinner, had to be immersed. Their baptism was simply a washing.

Hebrews 9:10, 13, 19, 21 are exceptionally clear. Baptist works on baptism do not give a satisfactory explanation of these verses. Alexander Carson is one of the best Baptist defenders of immersion; yet his discussion of these verses is lamentably weak. On one occasion a very good Baptist friend and a fine Biblical student when asked how he interpreted these verses changed the subject and did not reply. Of course, Carson's poor attempt, and the failure to find a better Baptist attempt are not conclusive. But the verses in Hebrews are conclusive.

In Greek the divers washings of Hebrews 9:10 are divers *baptisms*. Let everyone check for himself. Even if one cannot read Greek, he can see that the word begins with b, and the third letter is the algebraic sign for pi. There are a t and an i easily recognizable. The whole word therefore is baptisms. These washings were of course purifications. Now, all the purifications mentioned in this chapter of Hebrews were performed by sprinkling. Some of these sprinklings were sprinklings of blood. Others were with water, as in verse 19. No doubt one of the Old Testament passages alluded to is Leviticus 14:50-52, where both blood and water were sprinkled. The passage in Hebrews then concludes with references to purging and purification. It follows therefore that the action of sprinkling can be referred to as a baptism.

After so much heavy argument, the discussion on the mode of baptism will have to be concluded with a bit of humor; though I trust it will not offend my good Baptist friends. In I Corinthians 10:1, 2 the Israelites are said to have been baptized in the cloud and in the sea. In I Peter 3:20 the flood is said to represent baptism. Now, while the Israelites and Noah may have been sprinkled a little, it was the others who were immersed.

The conclusion here is that Scripture nowhere requires immersion; that no clear cases of immersion are described; that sprinkling and pouring were common; and hence to insist on immersion is to add to God's requirements.

The second point listed above was a minor one: Who should administer the rite? Anyone? Even a heretic or pagan? Or only an ordained minister? The answer to this question depends largely on the efficacy of baptism. Rome, and with qualifications the Lutherans also, hold that baptism produces regeneration. Rome makes baptism absolutely essential to salvation, and invents a place, neither heaven nor hell, for infants who die unbaptized. Hence Rome allows anyone, pagans or heretics, to baptize. If the Lutherans rule out pagans and heretics, they at least allow any Christian believer, including women, to perform the rite.

The Calvinists usually frown on lay baptism. Since Christ appointed a form of government for his church, and since he indicated the election of officers to administer its ordinances, the regularly ordained minister is the proper person to perform the rites. It is reported that the Huguenots, during the terrible sufferings of their persecution, having no ordained ministers, went for years without the sacraments. Or, running great danger, they would try to smuggle a young candidate for the ministry out to Geneva for ordination and then smuggle him back again. But the Scottish Presbyterians held that exceptional circumstances may cautiously call for irregular procedures. Thus Charles Hodge (*Systematic Theology,* Vol. III, p. 525) says, "for any man, under ordinary circumstances, not duly appointed, to assume the functions of the ministry, is irregular and wrong." The wording seems to allow irregularities in extraordinary circumstances. In fact, what is worse than lay baptisms, some Puritans, in prison and about to be executed, celebrated the Lord's Supper alone. We honor and sympathize with the martyrs; but the sacraments, especially the Lord's Supper, are congregational affairs, requiring the preaching of the Word. It is therefore strange that a Puritan, facing martyrdom under Bloody Mary, should follow the Romish invention of private communion.

The third of the four questions now is: To whom should baptism be administered? This question also divides in two. Should unbelievers be baptized or believers only? And, should infants be baptized or adults only?

In the New Testament, so far as adults are concerned, the practice and the teaching were to baptize on confession of faith: Repent and be baptized. The Philippian jailer and all his family were baptized straightway after he asked, "What must I do to be saved?" This is a far cry from the Romish practice of baptizing the heathen in crowds, as for example upon the conversion of Clovis, or apparently upon the conversion of no one in Buddhist lands.

At the same time, it must be noted that the apostles gave very little Christian instruction. The Jews at Pentecost knew the Old Testament and needed only to learn that Jesus was their Messiah; but the jailer surely knew little if anything, yet he and his household were baptized after one sermon. The next day Paul left the city. Later in church history there were catechetical classes, lasting a few months or even a few years. Though this bears the appearance of wisdom, it was not the practice of the apostles. Yet they certainly required a profession of faith.

The second half of this sub-question also divides into two: Should infants ever be baptized, and if so, which infants?

The basic authority for baptizing infants is found in the terms of the Abrahamic covenant. Infants, male infants, were circumcised. Now, as the Lord's Supper grew out of and replaced the Passover meal, so baptism replaced circumcision. The most definite passage on the subject is Colossians 2:11, 12 where baptism is called the circumcision of Christ. The less definite but more pervasive material concerns the continuance of the Abrahamic covenant, as found in Galatians 3:15ff.

In this connection one should note that it is not necessary to find explicit New Testament justification for every Christian doctrine. The Old Testament is a part of the Bible also. To be sure, the Mosaic ritual was a temporary expedient. To continue the sacrifice of lambs today would be to deny the efficacy of Christ's sacrifice. But while the ritual is fulfilled, the covenant of grace remains the same in all ages. A relatively minor, though for that very reason pertinent, point concerns the condemnation of incest in I Corinthians 5:1ff. The New Testament gives no details concerning the limits of consanguinity and affinity in marriage. They are found in Leviticus 18. See I Corinthians 1:19, 31; 2:9, 16; 3:19, 20; 6:16; 9:9; 10:7 and others, plus frequent verbal allusions that cannot quite be called quotations in the modern sense. In chapter five, however, Paul does not quote Leviticus but clearly Leviticus is the only place that affords Paul a basis for his condemnation. The correct principle of interpretation is not the Baptist one of discarding everything in the Old Testament not reasserted in the New; but rather the acceptance of everything in the Old not abrogated by New Testament teaching.

Therefore to be more explicit, be it noted that the Old Testament church and the New Testament church are the same church. Not only does Acts 8:38, "the church in the wilderness" so assert, but even clearer is Romans 11:17-24. There was a root; one of its branches was Israel; this branch was broken off; a Gentile branch from a wild olive tree was grafted into the good root; and God can and will at some future date graft back the natural branches into their own olive tree. The whole, as Galatians 6:16 indicates, is the Israel of God. Since, now, children were members of the ancient church, and were given the sign of the covenant, so also now.

Anyone who wishes to exclude infants from the church is under obligation to show that the New Testament alters the procedure that dates back at least to Abraham. It is the Baptist who must bear the burden of proof. He must explain how it comes about that children, who were members of the church before the time of Christ, are now excluded from the church. All other Christians are satisfied with the household baptisms of Acts 16:15, the jailer in Acts 16:33, and the household of Stephanus in I Corinthians 1:16.

The other subdivision of the question is a more difficult one: Whose children should be baptized? It is not at all difficult to show that a child of two believing parents should be baptized, nor even that a child of only one believing parent should be. I Corinthians 7:14 is sufficient. The difficulty arises when one considers the case of a child whose parents were perhaps baptized in infancy, who attend church services with some regularity, and who want their child baptized, even though they themselves have never become communicant members. Today in the United States the very large majority who are in regular attendance are communicant members. But it so happens that regular attendants who are not communicants want their children baptized. Should the church acquiesce?

In Europe and in early America the children of baptized but non-communicant members were regularly baptized. Robert Ellis Thompson, in *A History of the Presbyterian Churches in the United States* (1895, p. 14) reports: "The absence of regularly constituted sessions for the administration of church discipline, and the refusal of baptism to the children of baptized persons who were not communicants, marked the local congregation as un-Presbyterian." That is, communicant membership was not essential for the parents of infants to be baptized; and the author notes that this was the rule in all the Reformed churches.

The argument was that there is a visible and an invisible Church. The members of the latter are precisely God's elect; but many members of the former are not. Ishmael and Esau were both circumcised. Furthermore, since the promise and covenant extend to a thousand generations, the visible church today may and ought to baptize infants of unbelieving parents who want them baptized, on the basis of their ancestors' faith. Surely not every Israelite, at any period of its disappointing history, was regenerate; yet no priest would have hesitated to circumcise the children of such parents. But in New England, as was not true in Europe, an inference drawn with respect to the Lord's Supper deserves mention at this point. Like baptism, the sacrament of the Lord's Supper came to be regarded as a sacrament of the visible church. The grandfather of Jonathan Edwards argued that regeneration is not a necessary qualification for admission to the Lord's Supper. In fact the sacrament itself is a converting ordinance. Increase Mather opposed this view; Jonathan Edwards in time came to oppose it also, for which cause he was dismissed from the pastorate he had inherited from his grandfather. Presbyterians generally followed Mather and Edwards in this regard.

Now, even if it be granted that baptism may properly be administered to children of non-professing parents, the inference to a similar stance on the Lord's Supper is fallacious. The two sacraments should be distinguished. The distinction is this: Admitting for the sake of argument that the covenant extends to thousands of generations, one must still remember that the apostle commanded each person to examine himself and so let him eat, on pain of eating and drinking damnation to himself. Obviously Paul did not intend the Supper to be a converting ordinance. The radical individualism of regeneration prevails.

But now, beyond admissions for the sake of argument, what must be said on the substantial question? Does the Bible require or prohibit baptisms to the thousandth generation? If it does, and if a generation is roughly thirty years, a thousand generations from the time of Christ would include just about everybody in the western world. Then the church should have baptized the child of an intensely Talmudic Jew whose ancestor in 50 B.C. was piously looking for the Messiah. Or, George Whitefield should have baptized Thomas Jefferson, Benjamin Franklin, and Tom Paine, as children, because one of their ancestors played a small role in the Reformation. Strange as this may seem to many, it ought to have been done if the Bible so teaches.

Some very eminent theologians have so held. The strictest view has not been universal; it is more American than European. The view that only the children of professing parents should be baptized seems to have been the result of colonial revivalism. An historian might care to determine whether Tennant was its originator. In those days, as also in the early twentieth century, the Presbytery of New York was lax in doctrine, while the Philadelphia Presbytery was noted for orthodoxy. Gilbert Tennant, pastor in New Brunswick, New Jersey, too vigorously castigated the Philadelphia ministers for their dead orthodoxy. This led Synod to condemn Tennant on charges of slander and to exclude him with one of his associates from the Synod. Tennant eventually repented, but at the moment the New Brunswick Presbytery withdrew from the Synod and the New York Presbytery followed them. The Synod then tightened its ordination vows, which from the Adopting Act of 1729 allowed candidates for ordination to state their scruples or disagreements with the Confession. The Synod now required unconditional subscription.

There was a strange mixture of ideas in the minds of these revivalists. In theology they were more lax than the Philadelphia ministers were; but they were more strict with reference to baptism. But though strange, it is understandable. Their pietism and evangelistic zeal led them to place great emphasis on conversion as a traumatic experience. Zeal in preaching false doctrine was better than preaching the truth without zeal. Let it be noted that this was not the case with Whitefield. He preached the truth with zeal. He did not, however, use a mourner's bench or a sawdust trail. Tennant, on the other hand, can be called the forerunner of Finney—that disaster which Christianity suffered in the next century—though of course, being a century earlier, Tennant was far more orthodox than Finney.

This emotional pietism, as it demanded a particular type of experience for regeneration, tended to view the ideal church as consisting entirely of regenerate persons sharing such an experience. The logical result is the Baptist position; but in Presbyterianism it stopped short at requiring faith of the parents who wanted their children baptized. But if it did not result in Baptist practices, it involved a change in the theology of baptism. This now is the fourth question: What is the meaning of baptism and what does the rite accomplish?

The Presbyterian position is neither Baptist nor Anglican, and of course not Romish. The discussion of the older view, that of baptismal regeneration, will come first.

One of the verses used to support baptismal regeneration is John 3:5: "Unless one is begotten of water and Spirit, he cannot enter the Kingdom of God." Does this mean that the rite of baptism produces regeneration and that no one without water baptism can enter heaven? An examination of the context can alone give the answer.

Point one: Nicodemus was a Jew, honestly seeking the truth. Therefore Jesus, in explaining the earlier phrase "unless a man is born over again, he cannot see the Kingdom of God," had to appeal to what Nicodemus already knew, *i.e.*, the Old Testament. Jesus could not assume that Nicodemus knew something foreign to the Old Testament. This is not the surmise of a modern theologian: It is the plain meaning of verse 10: "Art thou the [outstanding] teacher of Israel and knowest not these things?" Clearly Jesus was basing his teaching on the Old Testament.

Point two: Therefore the meaning of *water* must be determined by the Old Testament. In the Christian era water might suggest baptism, Christian baptism, but in the historical circumstances the preceding usage is what was meant, not something later about which Nicodemus had had no opportunity to learn. Now, the previous usage differs from the later in several respects: It was not Trinitarian; it could be repeated, even several times, whereas Christian baptism is administered just once.

Point three: In the Old Testament baptism or washing with water symbolizes cleansing from sin. In Isaiah 4:4 the Lord *washed* away the filth of the daughters of Zion; Zechariah 13:1 mentions a *fountain* for sin and impurity; Malachi 3:2 predicts a purification, by fire indeed, but also by *soap*, which no doubt requires water. Then further, the combination of water and spirit in John has its background in many Old Testament passages. Psalm 51:2, 7, 10 combine the washing, a clean heart, and a right spirit. Isaiah 44:3 also.

Point four: The Kingdom of God is also something Nicodemus should have understood. It is an Old Testament idea, for God is King. The term itself does not occur in I Chronicles 29:11, but the idea is emphatic. Explicit are:

> Psalm 22:28: For the kingdom is the Lord's and he is the governor among the nations.
> Psalm 45:6: Thy throne, O God, is for ever and ever: the sceptre of thy kingdom is a right sceptre.
> Psalm 145:11: They shall speak of the glory of thy kingdom, and talk of thy power.

To these add Isaiah 24:23, Daniel 2:44 and many other references. Since such passages teach about the Kingdom, one can at least hope to find, in the Old Testament, the conditions of membership in that Kingdom. The conditions are repentance, faith, trust, sacrifice, redemption, the new heart, the Spirit—all gospel terms. Is it then peculiar that *water* should be there also?

The conclusion is that Jesus was teaching the Old Testament to Nicodemus, and that therefore there is no reference in John 3 to Christian baptism, and therefore again no theory of baptismal regeneration.

Another New Testament verse requires mention in this connection. Baptismal regeneration is sometimes supported by an appeal to Titus 3:5: "By the washing of regeneration and the renewing of [or, by] the Holy Spirit."

The Anglican and Romish argument is that washing regenerates. But this interpretation causes grammar to suffer. The second half of the quotation, in which *the Holy Spirit* is in the genitive case, obviously means that the Holy Spirit renews us. The Holy Spirit is a subjective genitive.

The Holy Spirit renews us; neither we nor anything else renew the Holy Spirit. The Holy Spirit cannot be the objective genitive. Similarly it is regeneration that does the washing; it is not the washing that washes regeneration. To get anything like baptismal regeneration out of these words, it would be necessary to rearrange them so as to say, "the regeneration of washing." This would mean that regeneration is produced by washing. But this is the reverse of what the Apostle wrote. Therefore the Reformed churches in baptizing adults assume, even if mistakenly, that they have already been regenerated. On this understanding regeneration cannot be conceived as produced by the rite of baptism.

If the preceding is a sufficient refutation of baptismal regeneration, the Baptist position will not so much require a formal refutation as a positive statement of the Presbyterian view. Baptists regard baptism as a sign of regeneration; and regeneration is to be recognized by a profession of faith. Presumably most Baptists would admit that the Holy Spirit can regenerate infants, and some no doubt concede that he does. Luke 1:44 says that the babe in the womb of Elizabeth leaped for joy when the mother of the Lord came to visit them. Contemporary murderous abortionists do not like this verse. Of course a newly born infant cannot express his faith. No matter, say the Lutherans, infants can and some infants do have faith because some infants are justified and justification is by faith alone. This is an impressive argument; but Presbyterians, thinking of a theological expression of faith, allow other means of justification for the incompetent exceptions such as infants and the insane. The Baptists do not allow these exceptions, neither do they allow for faith in infants, and hence they will not baptize them.

Some Presbyterians claim to baptize infants on the basis of "presumptive regeneration." "Presumptive election" would be a better basis. But this is only a partial answer to the main question.

That baptism, the sign of washing and purification, is somehow related to regeneration should not be denied; but the Baptist view of that relationship is untenable. They rebel at the apparently empty formalism of the established churches in Europe. They observe that too many "baptized" infants give no later evidence of regeneration or election, which is unfortunately true. But neither Tennant's ideal of a regenerate ministry, much less that of a regenerate membership, is possible. If this is true of churches that baptize infants, it is equally true and equally regrettable of churches that immerse adults. There are millions of apostate Baptists, with their champion of a generation ago, Harry Emerson Fosdick. Every church, with the possible exception of a few very small congregations, has its black sheep. This was the case in the churches of the New Testament and remains true today. Therefore it is impractical to operate on the belief, and impossible to operate on an asserted fact, that all church members are regenerate. Adult baptism does not avoid the difficulty.

The problem is solved by insisting that the New Testament gospel is the same as that given to Abraham. Baptism is the circumcision of Christ. The terms of the Abrahamic covenant provide the rules for the administration of baptism. The New Testament application of the covenant cannot be more restricted that that of the Old. In fact, it is wider, for girls are now baptized. Since therefore it is wider, not narrower, and since infants were then included in the covenant, they must not be excluded now.

That some or even many remain dead in sin after receiving the sign of the covenant, is no greater an objection to infant baptism than it is to circumcision. Ishmael and Esau bore the sign of the covenant. So too did Simon Magus and Hymenaeus, presumably unregenerate, or Diotrophes, Demas, Alexander, and others who made shipwreck of the faith.

In spite of the fact that they are criticizing the divine provisions of the Abrahamic covenant, so definitely said to be operative today (Galatians 3:7ff), Baptists and others will ask, "But, then, what good is baptism?" Of course one might ask in return, "What good is adult immersion? It does not regenerate, and some of you deny it is a means of grace. What then is left?"

Now, Presbyterians can answer these questions better than Baptists can. To repeat, baptism has all the value of circumcision.

> Romans 2:25: For circumcision verily profiteth, if thou keep the law: but if thou be a breaker of the law, thy circumcision is made uncircumcision.
>
> Romans 3:1, 2: What advantage then hath the Jew? Or what profit is there of circumcision? Much every way: chiefly, because that unto them were committed the oracles of God.
>
> Romans 4:11: And he received the sign of circumcision, a seal of the righteousness of the faith which he had yet being uncircumcised: that he might be the father of all them that believe, though they be not circumcised: that righteousness might be imputed unto them also.

Doubtless this is not so much value as some might expect. But if so, these expectations are not Scriptural. Perhaps the Calvinist must say that while baptism symbolizes internal blessings, it guarantees only external.

However, this is still a means of grace, *i.e.*, something God uses to show us his favor. For one reason, the rite, entered into sincerely, helps to fix the Word in the convert's mind. The Word is necessary. Baptism is not a magic incantation. It does not exercise "physical causality," as the

Catholic Encyclopedia describes it, referring to Thomas Aquinas, *Summa Theologica* (3a62); a physical causality such that "the sacramental rite is directly involved in the infusion of grace in a manner analogous to that in which an instrument, such as a pen or brush, is said to be the cause of an effect, the written page or picture." No, the rite of baptism, though a visible performance, requires understanding, intelligence, mind.

When God made his covenant with Abraham, in Genesis 17, he explained its terms. There are approximately nine verses of explanation before circumcision is mentioned. Then follow five verses explaining circumcision. To this is added the promise of a son to Sarah. Here something peculiar appears: The covenant will be established in his son Isaac, not in Ishmael; nevertheless Abraham circumcised Ishmael, along with servants who had been bought with money and were not of his family. Thus at the initiation of the rite there was explanation. In Joshua 5:2-9 where the uncircumcised second generation are circumcised, there is no explicit mention of an explanation to these people; the book explains the event to its readers; but it is almost impossible that Joshua would or could do this on a nation-wide scale without giving them an explanation. Thus the minister today must explain its significance to those who present themselves. Even the Philippian jailer, baptized so suddenly, received some instruction; and what was lacking in time was more than compensated for by the preceding miracle. Baptism pictures the washing away of sin by Christ's blood. We are baptized into his death, as the Baptists are fond of repeating. This is true; but it is incomplete: We are baptized in the name of the Trinity, not just Christ's death alone. This must be explained. The rite itself presents the promise of the covenant in the form of an action. As a picture of the washing away of sin, baptism is a "visible word." Now, the difference between the audible and the visible Word is this: The word is preached in general terms to everyone. Baptism is administered to this one individual person here and now, showing him that the covenant is not merely some corporate arrangement in general, but showing him that God gives to him individually the promises of the covenant. This is absent when baptism is not accompanied by the Word, or where the words are Latin which the people do not understand.

The Protestant Reformation was a tremendous break with the encrusted superstitions of a thousand years. It is no derogation to the Reformers to suggest that they did not completely wipe out every last trace of so entrenched a superstition. The Second Helvetic Confession seems to retain a bit in its words, "*Nam intus regeneramur*—in it we are regenerated." The French Confession of 1559 is better: "*parce que là nous sommes entés au corps de Christ, à fin d'être lavés et nettoyés par son sang* . . . by it we are grafted into the body of Christ, so as to be washed and cleansed by his blood. . . ." And then, "*Ainsi nous tenons que l'eau étant un élément caduc, ne laisse pas de nous testifier en verité le lavement intérieur de notre âme au sang de Jesus-Christ.*" In English: "Thus we hold that the water, though a powerless element, nevertheless truly testifies to us the internal washing of our soul by the blood of Jesus Christ."

The less important question of who may properly administer baptism can form a concluding paragraph on this subject and serve also as a transition to the discussion of the Lord's Supper.

Baptism and the Lord's Supper should be administered only by an ordained minister. One reason for this prescription is that God has appointed a government for his church, whose officers are lawfully called and presbyterially ordained. These officers are stewards of the mysteries of Christ: I Corinthians 4:1: "Let a man so account of us as of the ministers of Christ and stewards of the mysteries of Christ."

Paul was an apostle and a minister; Apollos and Sosthenes were ministers but not apostles. So too every minister is an ordained steward of God (Titus 1:5, 7). Consider also: Luke 12:42: "And the Lord said, Who then is that faithful and wise steward, whom his lord shall make ruler over his household, to give them their portion of meat in due season?"

This verse shows clearly that a steward is an officer appointed by the Lord to rule his household. There may be several wise, discreet, and trustworthy members of the household, but not all are stewards. The one appointed by the Lord has the function of portioning out the Lord's meat to the others. The others do not have that function. The following verses from Luke and Paul show that this divinely appointed government is to continue until the Lord's return.

> Acts 20:28: Take heed therefore unto yourselves, and to all the flock, over the which the Holy Ghost hath made you overseers, to feed the church of God, which he hath purchased with his own blood.
>
> Ephesians 4:11: And he gave some, apostles; and some, prophets; and some, evangelists; and some, pastors and teachers . . . .

Since the sacraments are means of grace, as the Word is, the work of a steward or minister is not only to preach but also to administer the sacraments. Thus the household is fed. The figure of speech, so frequent in the Scriptures, of sheep and shepherd shows that sheep need someone to feed them. They need to be led to green pastures. When they wander astray, various tragedies occur. But if any devout Christian may properly serve communion, the distinction between pastor and flock, between feeder and fed, is abolished. There may be some extenuating circumstances, as was the case with the Huguenots, when it might seem justifiable for a pious member to organize a communion service; but to put the Supper in the charge of a random member, however pious, when there are pastors easily available, as the anabaptists did, is a violation of God's appointments.

Not to extend the argument unduly, a conclusion or summary may be had by returning to Ephesians 4:11-13. The passage says that Christ gave some members of his body the function and office of apostle. Obviously he did not give this to many. He also gave to some the office of pastor and teacher. The purpose of these offices is to perfect the saints. Perfecting the saints includes the administration of the sacraments. This function was given to some, not to all.

The Lord's Supper

One of the major points of contention during the Protestant Reformation was the nature and effect of the Lord's Supper. This prominence did not depend merely on the general dispute about sacraments, but on the fact that this sacrament was celebrated in every local church every day. Each person was baptized just once in his lifetime; marriage might occur twice or even three times; but many peasants and every priest took communion daily. Hence a difference in administration here was much more visible to the populace than even the doctrine of justification by faith alone.

Since an earlier section discussed the nature of sacraments in general, there remain here the particular aspects of this sacrament.

The Shorter Catechism says:

Q. What is the Lord's Supper?
A. The Lord's Supper is a sacrament, wherein, by giving and receiving bread and wine, according to Christ's appointment, his death is showed forth: and the worthy receivers are, not after a corporal and carnal manner, but by faith, made partakers of his body and blood, with all his benefits, to their spiritual nourishment, and growth in grace.

The Lord's Supper represents a complex of ideas. The broken bread represents the broken body; the wine represents his poured out blood. But also as a supper or meal it also represents nourishment and a family friendship. By participating worthily we are assured of our union with Christ, of the forgiveness of sins, and of eternal life. Although Christ's sermon in John 6 was not an explanation of the Lord's Supper—because for one thing he was preaching to a hostile audience—yet the Supper is a symbol of the reality there announced.

Now, it happens that these simple ideas have, in the history of the visible church, been overlaid with major superstitions as well as with minor misunderstandings. The Baptists sometimes complain that infant baptism introduced many superstitious excrescences on the simple rite. While it is true that baptism was corrupted by the addition of non-scriptural ceremonies—though it is hard to show that infant baptism was their cause—the sacrament of the Lord's Supper became the occasion, not the cause, of still greater and more dangerous superstitions. We must therefore consider, chiefly, the differences among the Romish, Lutheran, and Reformed doctrines. These differences are not all of equal weight. One of the minor differences, whether or not the bread should be leavened or unleavened, can be disposed of first.

Probably no church absolutely forbids the use of

unleavened bread; but the Romish church requires, and some Protestant congregations regularly use, it. This practice has a Biblical plausibility, for no one denies that Christ and the disciples had to use unleavened bread. However, the fact that they had to use it—the divine regulations for the Jewish Passover required the removal of all leaven from every home—left them no choice. Had there been both leavened and unleavened bread on hand, and had Christ then chosen the unleavened bread, the example would have been normative for the church. But in the absence of a visible preference, the kind of bread used is a matter of indifference. Except insofar as the Puritan principle denies to the Church the authority to add requirements to or subtract requirements from the forms of worship, the use or non-use of unleavened bread is not so much a question of theology as a matter of curiosity.

The truly important point of contention is the Romish doctrine of transubstantiation. In conformity with the principle of sacramentarianism Rome takes the verse, "This is my body" as a literal, rather than as a figurative statement. "I am the door" is clearly figurative, since Christ is not a two inch thick wood panel. But Rome, and Luther too, insist that *Hoc est corpus meum* is literal.

Between Rome and Lutheranism there is a difference, of reasonable importance, which may be briefly mentioned and dropped. The Romish view is that when the priest miraculously turns the bread and wine into the literal body and blood of Christ, the change is permanent. And hence after the service they can put pieces and drops of God in a vase on the altar and bow or genuflect to it. The Lutherans restrict the effect of the priestly miracle to the duration of the service. Afterward only bread and wine remain, and the minister can take it home to dinner or feed it to the birds.

Some of the Protestant population wonder how bread can be literal flesh when it looks like, feels like, and tastes like bread. Rome has an answer to this objection. In keeping with Aristotelian philosophy, Rome distinguishes, with respect to all sensible objects, their substance from their qualities. Aristotle's basic categories of thought and reality were substance, quantity, quality, relation, position, affection, and some others. Transubstantiation means that the *substance* of the bread becomes flesh, while the *qualities* of the bread remain what they were.

The doctrine of transubstantiation was enforced by Pope Nicolas—and Popes are infallible in matters of doctrine—on Berengarius by prescribing, as his form of recantation, language to the effect that the body of Christ was locally present, felt by the hand, bruised by the teeth, and swallowed by the throat. Luther also said as much, though the Lutherans might not care to be so blunt. To support the local and physical presence of Christ's body in the bread, the Lutherans invented the doctrine of the *communicatio idiomatum*: i.e., that the human nature of Christ shares in the eternal attributes of Deity. Thus the physical body is omnipresent, and so there is enough of it to go around for all the communion services in the world. But once transubstantiation is admitted, the Romish view that the elements remain the literal body and blood seems more consistent than that the remaining body and blood fly back to heaven.

Those who stress the so-called literal meaning of the word *is*, or better, the literal meaning of the word *body*, and refuse to allow the bread to be the sign or symbol for the body, fall into inconsistency when they proceed to the other element. If the Scripture says that the bread is the body, it does not say that the wine is the blood. What Jesus said, and the words Paul reports, are "This cup is the new testament in my blood." Now, if one wish to insist on literal interpretation, it is not the wine but the cup, a silver vessel, that is—what? Not the blood of Christ, but the new testament in his blood. Hence a literal silver cup is literally the New Testament. One may also wonder whether a certain literal rock in the Sinai was literally Christ and whether that piece of stone locally and literally rolled along as the Israelites proceeded. Presumably the substance of the rock was turned into Christ himself, though it retained the qualities of hardness, shape, and texture it had before.

The distinction between substance and quality in the doctrine of transubstantiation might be taken as an amusingly fanciful application of Aristotelianism—it is certainly not Platonism—were it not that it entails the view that the Lord's Supper is a redemptive sacrifice, and that therefore it is a repetition of Calvary. But Scripture says:

> Hebrews 9:25-28: Nor yet that he must offer himself often, as the high priest [does with] the blood of others; for then must he often have suffered . . . but now *hapax* (once for all) . . . so Christ was offered *hapax* (once for all) to bear the sins of many.

Of all the evil inventions of Rome the most Satanic is the transubstantiation of the Lord's Supper into a sacrificial mass. The Romanists believe that the mass is a sacrifice by which we obtain from God the remission of our sins. Now, the passage from Hebrews just quoted occurs in a context that declares Christ to be a priest forever after the order of Melchizedek. The Mosaic priests served for a limited time —one high priest was succeeded by another. But Christ had no successors. This permanent priesthood renders unnecessary and indeed impossible any later priest who might claim to offer a sacrifice for sin. Therefore any man who claims to be a successor of Christ denies Christ's priesthood.

Of course the Romanists say that their mass does not abolish Christ's sacrifice, but merely repeats it, and that therefore the Romish priests do not supplant Christ, but merely assist him in the repetition. But Hebrews does not allow this evasion. Consider:

> Hebrews 7:23ff: Truly they were many priests . . . by reason of death. But this one [Jesus], because he remains forever, has an unchangeable priesthood . . . who has no need, as the [previous] high priests had, of offering a sacrifice day after day . . . . For this he did just once (*ephapax*) when he offered himself.

The point is that there were many Jewish priests because the death of one necessitated the administrations of another. But Christ's death did not put an end to his priesthood, and therefore he has no successors. The claim to be a successor to Christ in the priestly office is to claim that death ended Christ's priesthood.

Furthermore, if the mass is a sacrifice is to atone for our sins, then the cross of Christ is denied its power. The Romanists have altars in their churches. They are erected in contact with the back wall so that no one can stand between the altar and the wall. The Reformed Episcopal denomination and a few particular Protestant Episcopal congregations require the communion table to be far enough away from the wall as to permit the minister to stand behind it. This is to show that the table is not an altar. A church that has an altar substitutes itself for the cross on Calvary. But if Christ has secured eternal redemption for us, and saves us "to the uttermost" (*eis to panteles* = completely, wholly, for all time), reliance on a later sacrifice denies the effectiveness of Christ. Christ said, It is finished; Rome says, We will finish it for him.

The anti-scriptural implications of the mass are many. Here is one more. The Lord's Supper is a Thanksgiving service: It is called the *eucharist*. In it we receive nourishment from God and thank him for his mercies. But the mass is not something God gives to us, it is a sacrifice we give to

God for the expiation of our sins. In the Lord's Supper God gives and we receive; in the mass man gives and God is supposed to receive. Now, if the mass is a sacrifice, the idea of communion, if not obliterated, is degraded; for a sacrifice-mass can be offered by just one person, *i.e.*, private masses without a communing congregation. Mass therefore changes communication into excommunication, as Calvin neatly puts it, for the priest separates himself to eat and drink by himself.

The Reformed theologians to a greater degree than the Lutherans corrected the impiety of the mass. In the historical situation it was necessary for them, not only to point out how the Papists contradicted Scripture, but positively to explain what the Scriptures taught.

The learned volumes on Systematic Theology usually at this point offer some objections to the views of Zwingli. This Swiss Reformer actually antedated Luther's ninety-five theses by a year or so. He is often represented as describing the Lord's Supper as a memorial service *and nothing more.* Calvin insisted on something more. The *Institutes* (IV xvii 18) say, "not a mere reception of it in the imagination or apprehension of their mind, but a real enjoyment of it as the food of eternal life." By this and similar expressions Zwingli's view is usually adjudged defective and Calvin's more complete. However, the difficulty is to determine what Calvin meant by "something more." One readily agrees that the value of the Lord's Supper does not reside in the recipient's having a visual image of the scene on Calvary. A mere visual image has no intellectual content. But why cannot the value of the sacrament be located in the "apprehension of their mind"? Paul says we are to examine ourselves so as to discern the Lord's body. To *understand* that the bread is a symbol of Christ's broken body, and to understand further what Christ actually accomplished on the cross, is surely more than to have a visual image. Why should not this apprehension of the mind be the factor by which the sacrament takes effect in the believer? How else could it take effect? When Calvin says, *not* the apprehension of the mind, but a real enjoyment of it as food, he drops from literal statement to figurative. What is meant by *food*? Are we not nourished or edified by *understanding* the significance of the sacrament?

Now, Zwingli is often berated for reducing the Lord's Supper to a "mere" memorial service. But it is hard to explain a memorial of Christ's death that is nothing more. Surely participation in such a service produces some spiritual result. Even in human affairs Memorial Day produces or reproduces, perhaps faintly in these later years, some clearer notion of good citizenship. When therefore Zwingli acknowledged that the sacraments were intended to be significant emblems of the great truths of the Gospel, and that they were intended to teach these truths, it is hard to see how anyone can deny that teaching is a means of grace. When he also says, "It is impossible that anything external should stabilize or confirm the internal faith of a man," he may be thinking of *ex opere operato,* the mere external motions. Teaching and significance can be truly called internal. Charles Hodge himself, after his moderate but negative remarks on Zwingli, says, "On this subject [the source of the sacrament's power] it is taught [by the Reformed doctrine] negatively that the virtue is not in them."

Hodge seems to think that Zwingli reduced the sacraments to the level of the rainbow: "They were to him no more means of grace than the rainbow or the heaps of stones on the banks of the Jordan. By their significancy and by association they might suggest truth and awaken feeling, but they were not channels of divine communication" (Vol. III, p. 499).

Maybe a little caution is needed here. In the first place neither the rainbow nor the Lord's Supper is in the strictest sense a communication from God. The first communication was made verbally to Noah and the second to the apostles. The signs or symbols can be understood only by those who have received the verbal revelation. Of course the two communications differ in content. One is a promise not to destroy the world by a second flood. Surely Zwingli did not reduce the Lord's Supper to the level of the rainbow. But though the two communications differ in this important respect, they are both means of grace. Looking at the rainbow reminds us of God's promise and so edifies us and renews our faith. So too does the Lord's Supper—with its more important message of course.

Then too, three pages later, Hodge's truly excellent statement does not seem to go beyond Zwingli's thought:

> There is therefore, a strict analogy, according to the Reformed doctrine, between the Word and the sacraments as means of grace. (1) Both have in them a certain moral power due to the truth which they bring before the mind. (2) Neither has in itself any supernatural power to save or to sanctify. (3) All their supernatural efficiency is due to the cooperation or attending influence of the Holy Spirit. (4) Both are ordained by God to be the channels or means of the Spirit's influence, to those who by faith receive them. Nothing is said in the Bible to place the sacraments above the Word as a means of communicating to men the benefits of Christ's redemption. On the contrary, tenfold more is said in Scripture of the necessity and efficiency of the Word in the salvation of men, than is therein said or implied of the power of the sacraments. (Vol. III, p. 502).

Now, it may be that the present writer is too generous

toward Zwingli, but it is also possible that some later Calvinists have demanded from him statements more explicit than those he wrote. Since Zwingli rose on the horizon at the very dawn of the Reformation, he was and had to be more concerned with his opposition to Rome than with the development of a greatly detailed theology. Thus his account may be truncated. Furthermore, we in later centuries, who have not faced his dangers, and with a language that has changed over the centuries, may not be able to judge his words aright.

At any rate Calvin would not reduce the Lord's Supper to a mere memorial service. To quote a more modern author, A.A. Hodge, *Outline of Theology,* says:

> Its truth [the truth of the Reformed view] as opposed to the meagre Zwinglian view . . . is established as follows: (1) That the sacraments are not only signs of the grace of Christ, but also *seals* of the gospel covenant offering us that grace upon the condition of faith is evident from [Romans 4:11]. . . . the sacraments are the seals of that covenant. God in their appointment binds himself to the fulfilment of his promises. . . . (2) As seals attached to the covenant it follows that they actually convey the grace signified, as a legal form of investiture, to those to whom, according to the terms of the covenant, it belongs. Thus a deed, when signed and sealed, is said to convey the property it represents because it is the legal form by which the intention of the original possessor is publicly expressed, and his act ratified (pp. 596-597).

That this differs from the "meagre" Zwinglian view, A.A. Hodge substantiates by a quotation from Limborch:

> It remains to say that God, through the sacraments, exhibits to us his grace, not by conferring it in

fact through them, but by representing it and placing it before our eyes through them as clear and evident signs. . . . And this efficacy is no other than objective, which requires a cognitive faculty rightly disposed that it may be able to apprehend that which the sign offers objectively to the mind. . . . They operate upon us as signs representing to the mind the thing whose sign they are. No other efficacy ought to be sought for in them (p. 602).

Limborch here uses the term *exhibit*, which term Hodge emphasizes as strictly Calvinistic: "It is evident that the term *exhibit* has retained in our standards the former sense of *conveying, conferring*. As in medical language, 'to exhibit a remedy' is to administer it" (p. 591). Yet Limborch was an Arminian of the late seventeenth and early eighteenth centuries. Dorner, *A System of Christian Doctrine* (translated by Cave and Banks, 1882; Vol. IV, p. 317), says, "In his last years Zwingli returned to his former standpoint, according to which the Holy Supper is not merely a sign of a past thing and commemoration thereof, but a means of grace and present gift."

Part of the difficulty in this matter is the figurative language, if not in the term *sign*, at least in the term *seal*. But even if the strictly legal use of a seal (now generally abandoned, in this country at least) is emphasized, it is not the seal itself—a piece of wax or an ink stamp—but the content of the document that is determinative. Limborch may mean no more than this. Zwingli apparently was willing to accept the phrase "a means of grace." Yet Hodge does not like this. He seems to think that Zwingli's view prevents the sacrament from being a means of grace, for he says in disparagement, "Thus the sacraments are *only* effective means of the objective presentation of the truth symbolized" (p. 591).

Yet why cannot an effective means of presenting the

truth be a means of grace? At this point Hodge seems to echo, perhaps faintly, but nonetheless seems to echo some of the Romish magic. To the contrary, the Bible places the value of the sacrament on a strictly intellectual or intelligible level. It is no magic. The believer must examine himself and be convinced once again that he understands what he is doing. He must believe the doctrine he understands. He must discern the significance, or eat damnation to himself.

Perhaps some of these earlier writers missed or underestimated a distinction that many people hardly think of. The distinction is that between the elements on the Lord's table, or Romish altar, and the communicants' partaking of them. When the Romanists claimed that the elements are transmuted into literal flesh and blood, reserved on the altar and bowed to, it was salutary to insist that they are mere signs. But when the devout believer—not a person who does not believe in them—partakes of them, there comes into play all that the recipient understands. Thus since the communicant deliberately, intentionally, and understandingly partakes, the service becomes a means of grace. How could it be otherwise? For the preaching of the Word itself, even apart from the sacrament, is also a means of grace.

Sanctification, the Christian life, the life and organization of the church involve more than the two sacraments, and more in particular than the general principle of perseverance. The Westminster Confession has chapters on Religious Worship and the Sabbath Day, Lawful Oaths and Vows, the Civil Magistrate, Marriage and Divorce, the Church (ordination, elders, deacons), Church Censures, Synods and Councils. In addition to these chapters in the confession, there are volumes and volumes on these subjects. But perhaps the junior in seminary will agree to forgo them until next year.

6. The Christian Life

The title of this section, The Christian Life, is somewhat peculiar because the preceding sections, Assurance,
Perseverance, Sacraments, are as much parts of the Christian life as anything else. The section on the sacraments has
shown that attendance upon the Lord's Supper is a means
of grace and a part of sanctification. Regular church
attendance is also a means of grace. Here there is a peculiar
difference between American customs and European in
this matter. In the United States, if because of illness or
carelessness, people are lax in weekly attendance, they
make a special effort to be present for the sacrament, with
the result that the congregation is usually larger on
communion Sunday than on other Sundays. In Europe it is
the other way around. Fewer people participate in the
Lord's Supper. In fact I have seen and heard the minister, at
L'Oratoire in Paris, dismiss the general congregation and
invite those who wish, to gather forward for communion.
At least three-quarters of the congregation left. So did I, but
presumably not for the same reason. Though I attended the
church as a recognition of St. Bartholomew's Massacre, I
did not wish to join in a thoroughly liberal communion
service. Few who walked out could have had the same
reason. Perhaps they held communion in greater awe, and
themselves as more unworthy, than Americans do. Yet
even some Americans do. Once I inveigled a school chum
of mine, in later life, to accompany me to church one
Sunday morning. As I was only visiting the city, I was
unaware that they would celebrate the Lord's Supper. My
chum had been raised by fairly conscientious Presbyterian
parents, but had, unfortunately, long ceased church attendance. When the elements were passed, he whispered that
he had been taught that participation required some

preparation through the preceding week, and that therefore he would not partake. If only more of his early training had survived! However, the Christian life includes other activities also.

The regular worship of God in the ordinary church services is one of these activities. Christ's words, "Thou shalt worship the Lord thy God, and him only shalt thou serve" (Matthew 4:10), very obviously are not restricted to the weekly worship service. They have to do with daily temptations. But they apply to Sunday also. Hebrews 10:25 says, "Stimulate one another to good deeds, not forsaking the assembling of yourselves together, as the manner of some is."

Perhaps it is not necessary to dwell on the nature and excellencies of Deity which not merely justify but which command our obeisance. These attributes have been largely examined in my book on the Trinity. Here it must suffice merely to mention omnipotence, omniscience, and omnipresence as reasons for acknowledging God's transcendent glory by our worship. They are so overwhelming, when one pauses to consider them, and so awe-inspiring, that many theologians, for this and other considerations, stress God's incomprehensibility. But in doing so, some of them distort the truth. If the divine incomprehensibility means that we do not know, and cannot know, everything that God knows, there can be no objection. This truth is all too comprehensible. But in an attempt to glorify God, some theologians exaggerate incomprehensibility and make God utterly unknowable. The mystics are the most consistent on this point: Barth makes God the "totally other"; but there are also some who even clearly assert that God can be known, and yet so emphasize incomprehensibility as to contradict their more orthodox assertions. One such theologian, who indeed uses the phrase "thinking God's thoughts after him," denies the phrase in another place by insisting that God's knowledge and the knowledge possible to man do not coincide at any single point. Consequently if God knows that David was king of Israel, we cannot know it. Indeed, since God knows everything, we can know nothing at all, for there is not a single point of coincidence between his knowledge and what we call our knowledge. But an essential part of divine worship is to know God and to know him correctly. That is why God has given us a revelation. What good is a revelation if it does not give us understandable truths? How can we praise God by singing "Lord God Almighty," if we do not know that God is Almighty? In a context where one would hardly expect a recommendation of intellectualism, Isaiah 33:6 says, "Wisdom and knowledge shall be the stability of thy times and strength of salvation." One can never worship the God of truth by deprecating the intellect. Acceptable worship of God, as an important part of sanctification, requires knowledge.

What in this context seems to need more emphasis than the attributes of God is the negative proposition that there must be no other object of worship. Few Americans worship graven images, though only by devious definitions do Romanists claim to avoid such idolatry. In fact, not only does the Bible condemn three dimensional statues, but Numbers 33:52 includes pictures as well. In apostolic times some people began to worship angels, and though this is more plausible than a worship of images, or even of the sun, let alone snakes, Colossians 2:18 and Revelation 19:10, 22:9 forbid it. Indeed in the last two of these verses the angels themselves forbid it. Nor should any prayer be addressed to the Virgin Mary. All honor to the blessed Virgin, but she is of lower rank than the angels and she recognized the need of a Savior in Luke 1:47.

Ordinarily we in America do not think of avarice, gormandizing, or even pride in our exemplary character as idolatry; but Scripture does. Professional sports are the god of many Americans, and they worship them on every Lord's Day, as well as on Monday evening. Any activity which dominates our interest, has first place in our desires, and thus shuts God out, or reduces him to a secondary or tertiary status, is idolatry. Gormandizing, frequent in the Roman Empire, is not a particularly widespread sin in America, nor even gourmetizing; but Paul in his day could point to people whose god was their belly.

References to gluttony and baseball may serve to introduce the various virtues which God commands us to exercise. They are so numerous and are introduced more to fit the immediate needs of a particular congregation than to fit the need of a logical arrangement, that we must list them in a haphazard fashion. For example, II Peter 1:5-7 lists faith, virtue, knowledge, temperance, patience, godliness, brotherly love, kindness, and charity. Though not logically arranged and though not clearly distinguished one from another, for they overlap, one should realize that actions of these types, actions which non-christians imitate externally, are acts of worship. They are not sacraments, usually they are performed outside a church building, individual rather than congregational, but they are all worship. After writing eleven chapters of profound theology, Paul in Romans, chapters 12 to 14, and somewhat in the final two chapters, gives a list of virtues with more explanation than Peter gives.

Since the joys, the trials, the responsibilities, and exigencies of marriage occupy such a large proportion of an ordinary person's life, and since its origin was in Eden, not as a mere legal enactment or social convenience, but as a divine institution, and since in America at the end of this twentieth century divorce, homosexuality, and premarital sex are so largely destroying civilization, the Biblical principles need great emphasis. Marriage counselors generally, and occasionally even some Christan counselors, do not always give good advice.

One virtue, needed in marriage often more than elsewhere, is patience. Not only did Peter include it in his list, but I Thessalonians 1:3, I Timothy 6:11, Titus 2:2, Hebrews 10:36, and James 1:4, plus a dozen other verses also, encourage us to be patient. The trouble with counseling, however, is its difficulty in distinguishing between patience and shirking responsibility. On the other hand, what one wishes to call responsibility may appear to others as irresponsible harshness. Where Christians are persecuted by anti-christian governments, as was the case in ancient Rome, sixteenth century Europe, and in Cuba, Russia, and parts of Africa today, patience is more easily understood, if less easily practiced. Acts 14:22 teaches that "we must through many tribulations enter into the kingdom of God." Romans 12:12 tells us to persevere, endure, be patient in tribulations.

In spite of what some devotional writers say, I am not sure that patience is the correct response to Satanic temptations. Something more active seems requisite.

Hope is another virtue which advances one's degree of sanctification. Peter did not include it in the list quoted, but his two epistles mention it four times. The Bible, however, does not recommend hope *per se*. It is not concerned with a hope for a raise in salary or for a promotion in the company. Job 27:8 asks the rhetorical question, "What is the hope of the hypocrite, though he hath gained, when God taketh away his soul?" Or, (New American Standard Version) "What is the hope of the godless . . . ?" Even a hope of heaven may be evil, as it is when grounded in some supposed human merit. The really important thing is not the subjective experience, but the objective reality. Hope is virtuous only when directed toward godly ends. Several Psalms issue the command, "Hope thou in God." Psalm

71:5 says, "Thou art my hope, O Lord God." Jeremiah 17:7 assures us that "Blessed is the man that trusteth in the Lord, and whose hope the Lord is." In Colossians 1:27 Paul calls Christ "the hope of glory," and I Timothy 1:1 adds, "the Lord Jesus Christ, our hope." Hope in Christ includes, naturally, the hope to receive all his blessings. The references are so numerous, both in the Old Testament and the New, that it must suffice here to encourage the reader to look them up in a concordance.

Yet someone may say, Hope is indeed a virtue, and that the Bible sufficiently recommends it is undeniable; but how does one achieve, produce, or exercise it? I am despondent and everything happens for the worst. Rembrandt painted masterpieces, but that bit of information does not tell me how to paint. How then does one come to hope? To such a melancholy soul one may first give a rather peculiar answer and afterward something more intelligible. Assuming that the questioner is a Christian, and sincere, we can assure him that he already hopes, even if he is barely conscious of it. To believe in Christ is *ipso facto* to hope for salvation. One might alter a verse and say, Lord, I hope, help thou my hopelessness. Of course if he is not a Christian, he is without hope even though he has lively hopes. As was said before, it is the object not the subject that supplies the value. But there is also a second answer. It is: Study the Scripture. We grow in grace by increasing our knowledge. Gradually, not all at once, but slowly, by meditating on God's law both day and night, despondency will decrease and hope will increase. When Christian in his Pilgrimage was locked in the dungeon of Doubting Castle by Giant Despair, on the very night before he was to be killed he remembered he had a key that could unlock the prison doors. He just had not thought of it before, occupied as he was with his plight and its dangers. So as the sun was beginning to rise, he opened the door and ran. When Giant

Despair tried to chase him, the Giant fell down in an apoplectic fit.

Another Christian virtue, but one that is more contemned than praised, is zeal. The reason is that like hope there is a false zeal, that is, a zeal for the wrong object. False zeal, and often true zeal, in the eyes of the public is considerably worse than false hope. Examples of false zeal are Paul's zeal described in Philippians 3:6, "Concerning zeal, persecuting the church." In Romans 10:2 he notes that the Jews have a zeal for God, but not according to knowledge ". . . being ignorant of God's righteousness." The Judaizers in Galatia "zealously affect you, but not well" (Galatians 4:17). In the Old Testament too we find instances of false zeal. One of the most spectacular, though the word itself does not occur in the passage, is the frenzy of the priests of Baal in cutting themselves with knives and lancets till the blood gushed out. The Pharisees of Christ's time, and the Sadducees also, were zealous in plotting Christ's crucifixion.

But no matter how many examples of Satanic zeal may be found, it counts nothing against godly zeal. The difference lies not in the subjective emotion or volition, whichever it may be, but in the object. If our zeal is for the right object, we become imitators of God, for God himself is a jealous or zealous God (Exodus 20:5; Deuteronomy 4:24). See also II Kings 19:31, "The zeal of the Lord shall do this." Also, "They shall know that I the Lord have spoken it in my zeal, when I have accomplished my fury in them" (Ezekiel 5:13). Again, when Jesus cleansed the temple, the disciples were reminded of the verse, "The zeal of thine house hath eaten me up" (John 2:17). In Galatians 4:14-17 Paul refers to the zeal of the Judaizers and in contrast bears record that the true Christians would have plucked out their eyes and would have given them to him. Though the word *zeal* does not occur in verse 15, Paul concludes in verse 18, "It is good

always to be zealously affected in a good thing." In Titus
2:14 Paul explains that Christ gave himself to "redeem us
. . . and purify unto himself a peculiar people zealous of
good works."

Underlying the proper zeal for this or that immediate
object is, as the quoted verses show, a zeal for God. The
good works of Titus 2:14 require a knowledge of God and
his law. If we do not know what God has ordained as good,
we can do it only by ignorant accident; and the odds are
against the accident. True zeal for God must be a zeal for his
truth. Hence one who does not study God's Word should
be careful not to be zealous for anything. But with the Word
one must show zeal in the propagation of its message.

In this regard the visible church is sadly deficient.
Most of the large denominations are apostate. The fundamentalists may not be apostate, but they are inexcusably
inadequate. For example, an article entitled "Who Are the
'Real' Pseudo-Fundamentalists?" begins on page 10 of the
June 1983 issue of the *Fundamentalist Journal*. It is an attempt
to distinguish between real and pseudo-fundamentalists.
The two authors make a brief mention of the dozen small
books, *The Fundamentals*, which, published from 1909-1912,
popularized the term. The article defines real fundamentalists as those who subscribe to five points: the infallibility of
Scripture, the deity of Christ, his virgin birth, the substitu-
tionary atonement and the literal resurrection, and his literal
second coming. Pseudo-fundamentalists are those who,
though they may believe these five points, insist on adding
other doctrines until there are seven, or ten, or twenty, or
fifty fundamentals (p. 1, col. 2). "A pseudo-Fundamentalist
is then one who subtracts from or adds to these fundamentals" (p. 11, col. 1). Those who add to these five points "do
not represent the historical position of Fundamentalism"
(p. 11, col. 2).

If this were so, the contributors to *The Fundamentals*

could not have been fundamentalists because they added articles on the Lord's Day, regeneration, Satan, the Holy Spirit, the true church, prayer, future retribution, and some other items.

The article in the June issue does not include in its fundamentals the doctrine of the Holy Spirit, and only by a doubtful implication the doctrine of the Father. Hence the Trinity cannot be a fundamental doctrine of Christianity. Also missing are the doctrines of regeneration and sanctification. By their absence these doctrines are treated as additions. "Any one who demands more than this [list of five] is denying the historical roots of the movement," and is indulging in "denominational distinctives or personal biases" (p. 11, cols. 1 & 2).

Aside from eliminating the doctrines of the Trinity, regeneration, and sanctification, the article repudiates the Protestant Reformation. The two great points of the Reformation were *sola scriptura* and *sola fide*. The five points of fundamentalism, as these two authors define it, include *sola scriptura,* but they exclude justification by faith alone. This latter doctrine, however, is no unimportant excrescence. The Judaizers in Galatia believed all the five points of the article. They had accepted Jesus as their Lord and Messiah, they insisted on the infallibility of Scripture, and they looked forward to Christ's return. But of all the apostolic denunciations of heretics and false teachers Paul castigates the Judaizers more violently than any others. Why? Because they did not accept justification by faith alone. Justification by the Father, regeneration by the Spirit, plus the following sanctification are fundamental to Biblical religion, and without them there is no Christianity at all. Fortunately most fundamentalists indulge in some "denominational distinctives or personal biases."

In addition to zeal and hope, one could discuss, mainly by examples, Peter's list of virtues; but is it not obvious that the list has no logical arrangement and that the colloquial terms overlap? One of his items is "virtue," but is not virtue all-inclusive? And is not godliness also all-inclusive? Interesting anecdotes could be multiplied on each of these virtues, but their value for guidance is much overrated.

If one wish for a more logical and instructive formulation, the desire is fulfilled by the Ten Commandments. It is a mistake to restrict their authority to the so-called Mosaic dispensation. That God gave these commands to Adam and Eve long before he gave the tables of stone to Moses is clear from the fact that Cain was afraid his brothers would execute him for having murdered Abel. Neither murder nor secular disregard of God became evil for the first time after the Israelite slaves escaped from Egypt. In fact, the Egyptians themselves, pagan as they were, recognized murder and would have executed Moses, had they caught him. Obviously too, blood sacrifice, in anticipation of the Messiah, seems to have been instituted in Genesis 3:21, and was indubitably practiced by Noah (Genesis 8:20) and Abraham. These practices were procedures and progress in sanctification, but this is not the place to spend more time on ancient rites.

As the Ten Commandments were in effect before the time of Moses, so too they remain in effect after the resurrection of Christ. Here is the supreme document on sanctification. One of the excellencies of Calvinism is that Calvin emphasized them more than any theologian before him. Even though the Lutherans very commendably made a definite point of the three functions or uses of the Law, only the two Westminster Catechisms, of all the creedal formulations, give it such a detailed explanation. Since so many professed Christians know hardly anything about all this, I do not apologize for quoting the introductory section from the Larger Catechism. I am confident that the poorly instructed seminary graduate, if sincere, will, after reading it, be inspired to preach some sermons on the Law of God.

In addition to quoting four questions and answers, I have included, as samples, a few, only a few, of the Scriptural references appended to them.

Q. 96. What particular use is there of the moral law to unregenerate men?

A. The moral law is of use to unregenerate men, to awaken their consciences to flee from wrath to come,[b] and to drive them to Christ;[c] or, upon their continuance in the estate and way of sin, to leave them inexcusable,[d] and under the curse thereof.[e]

96. [b] 1 Timothy 1:9: Knowing this, that the law is not made for a righteous man, but for the lawless and disobedient, for the ungodly and for sinners, for unholy and profane, for murderers of fathers and murderers of mothers, for man-slayers, [10:] For whoremongers, for them that defile themselves with mankind, for men-stealers, for liars, for perjured persons, and if there be any other thing that is contrary to sound doctrine.

[c] Galatians iii. 24: Wherefore the law was our schoolmaster to bring us unto Christ, that we might be justified by faith.

[d] Romans i. 20: For the invisible things of him from the creation of the world are clearly seen, being understood by the things that are made, even his eternal power and Godhead; so that they are without excuse. Compare with Romans ii. 15: Which shew the work of the law written in their hearts, their conscience also bearing witness, and their thoughts the mean while accusing or else excusing one another.

[e] Galatians iii. 10: For as many as are of the works of the law are under the curse: for it is written, Cursed is every one that continueth not in all things which are written in the book of the law to do them.

Q. 97. What special use is there of the moral law to the regenerate?

A. Although they that are regenerate, and believe in Christ, be delivered from the moral law as a covenant of works, so as thereby they are neither justified nor condemned; yet, besides the general uses thereof common to them with all men, it is of special use, to shew them how much they are bound to Christ for his fulfilling it, and enduring the curse thereof in their stead, and for their good; and thereby to provoke them to more thankfulness, and to express the same in their greater care to conform themselves thereunto as the rule of their obedience.

Q. 98. Where is the moral law summarily comprehended?

A. The moral law is summarily comprehended in the ten commandments, which were delivered by the voice of God upon mount Sinai, and written by him in two tables of stone; and are recorded in the twentieth chapter of Exodus. The first four commandments containing our duty to God, and the other six our duty to man.

Q. 99. What rules are to be observed for the right understanding of the ten commandments?

A. For the right understanding of the ten commandments, these rules are to be observed:

1. That the law is perfect, and bindeth every one to full conformity in the whole man unto the righteousness thereof, and unto entire obedience for ever; so as to require the utmost perfection of every duty, and to forbid the least degree of every sin.[o]

2. That it is spiritual, and so reacheth the understanding, will, affections, and all other powers of the soul; as well as words, works, and gestures.[p]

3. That one and the same thing, in divers respects is required or forbidden in several commandments.[q]

4. That as, where a duty is commanded, the contrary sin is forbidden;[r] and, where a sin is forbidden, the contrary duty is commanded:[s] so, where a promise is annexed, the contrary threatening is included;[t] and, where a threatening is annexed, the contrary promise is included.[v]

5. That what God forbids, is at no time to be done;[w] what he commands, is always our duty;[x] and yet every particular duty is not to be done at all times.[y]

6. That under one sin or duty, all of the same kind are forbidden or commanded; together with all the causes, means, occasions, and appearances thereof, and provocations thereunto.[z]

7. That in what is forbidden or commanded to ourselves, we are bound, according to our places, to endeavor that it may be avoided or performed by others, according to the duty of their places.[a]

8. That in what is commanded to others, we are bound, according to our places and callings, to be helpful to them;[b] and to take heed of partaking with others in what is forbidden them.[c]

---

99. [o] Psalm xix. 7: The law of the Lord is perfect, converting the soul: the testimony of the Lord is sure, making wise the simple. James ii. 10: For whosoever shall keep the whole law, and yet offend in one point, he is guilty of all. Matthew v. 21: Ye have heard that it was said by them of old time, Thou shalt not kill; and whosoever shall kill shall be in danger of the judgment: [22:] But I say unto you, That whosoever is angry with his brother without a cause shall be in danger of the judgment; and whosoever shall say to his brother, Raca, shall be in danger of the council; but whosoever shall say, Thou fool, shall be in danger of hell-fire.

[p] Romans vii. 14: For we know that the law is spiritual; but I am carnal, sold under sin. Deuteronomy vi. 5: And thou shalt love the Lord thy God with all thine heart, and with all thy soul, and with all thy might. Compare with Matthew xxii. 37: Jesus said unto him, thou shalt love the Lord thy God with all thy heart, and with all thy soul, and with all thy mind. [38:] This is the first and great commandment. [39:] And the second is like unto it, Thou shalt love thy neighbour as thyself. Matthew v. 21, 22: [See letter [o].] [27:] Ye have heard that it was said by them of old time, Thou shalt not commit adultery: [28:] But I say unto you, That whosoever looketh on a woman to lust after her, hath committed adultery with her already in his heart. [33:] Again, ye have heard that it hath been said by them of old time, Thou shalt not forswear thyself, but shalt perform unto the Lord thine oaths: [34:] But I say unto you, Swear not at all: neither by heaven; for it is God's throne. [37:] But let your communication be, Yea, yea; Nay, nay: for whatsoever is more than these cometh of evil. [38:] Ye have heard that it hath been said, An eye for an eye, and a tooth for a tooth: [39:] But I say unto you, That ye resist not evil. [43:] Ye have heard that it hath been said, Thou shalt love thy neighbour, and hate thine enemy: [44:] But I say unto you, Love your enemies, bless them that curse you, do good to them that hate you, and pray for them which despitefully use you, and persecute you.

q Colossians iii. 5: Mortify therefore your members which are upon the earth; fornication, uncleanness, inordinate affection, evil concupiscence, and covetousness, which is idolatry. Amos viii. 5: Saying, When will the new moon be gone, that we may sell corn? and the sabbath, that we may set forth wheat, making the ephah small, and the shekel great, and falsifying the balances by deceit? Proverbs i. 19: So are the ways of every one that is greedy of gain; which taketh away the life of the owners thereof. 1 Timothy vi. 10: For the love of money is the root of all evil; which while some coveted after, they have erred from the faith, and pierced themselves through with many sorrows.

r Isaiah lviii. 13: If thou turn away thy foot from the sabbath, from doing thy pleasure on my holy day; and call the sabbath a delight, the holy of the Lord, honourable; and shalt honour him, not doing thine own ways, nor finding thine own pleasure, nor speaking thine own words.

7. Conclusion

After these introductory paragraphs there comes a long series of explanations, implications, and detailed applications of each commandment, on to Answer 151. Both the Catechism and the Westminster Confession emphasize that the moral law is useful as a guide to the Christian life and as the standard of Christian behavior, but righteousness does not come by the law. Our obedience to the law is the result, not the cause, of our growing sanctification. Let me conclude this treatise on sanctification by quoting first the apostle Paul, then the Westminster Confession of Faith, and finally Christ.

I have been crucified with Christ; it is no longer I who live, but Christ lives in me; and the life which I now live in the flesh I live by faith in the Son of God, who loved me and gave himself for me. I do not set aside the grace of God; for if righteousness comes through the law, then Christ died in vain.

What purpose then does the law serve? It was added because of transgressions, until the seed should

come to whom the promise was made. . . . Is the law
then against the promises of God? Certainly not! For if
there had been a law given which could have given
life, truly righteousness would have been by the law.

Chapter XIII of the Westminster Confession emphasizes the fact that we are sanctified by God, not by our own
efforts; our imperfect obedience to the moral law is a result
of that sanctification, not the cause of it. Sanctification
begins with regeneration.

They who were effectually called and regenerated, having a
new heart and a new spirit created in them, are further sanctified,
really and personally, through the virtue of Christ's death and
resurrection, by his Word and Spirit dwelling in them; the
dominion of the whole body of sin is destroyed, and the several
lusts thereof are more and more weakened and mortified, and
they more and more quickened and strengthened in all saving
graces, to the practice of true holiness, without which no man can
see the Lord.

This sanctification is throughout in the whole man, yet imperfect in this life: there abide still some remnants of corruption
in every part: whence ariseth a continual and irreconcilable war;
the flesh lusteth against the Spirit, and the Spirit against the flesh.

In which war, although the remaining corruption for a time
may much prevail, yet, through the continual supply of strength
from the sanctifying Spirit of Christ, the regenerate part doth
overcome: and so the saints grow in grace, perfecting holiness in
the fear of God.

"Sanctify them by your truth. Your word is truth."

Scripture Index

Index

The Crisis of Our Time

Historians have christened the thirteenth century the Age of Faith and termed the eighteenth century the Age of Reason. The twentieth century has been called many things: the Atomic Age, the Age of Inflation, the Age of the Tyrant, the Age of Aquarius. But it deserves one name more than the others: the Age of Irrationalism. Contemporary secular intellectuals are anti-intellectual. Contemporary philosophers are anti-philosophy. Contemporary theologians are anti-theology.

In past centuries secular philosophers have generally believed that knowledge is possible to man. Consequently they expended a great deal of thought and effort trying to justify knowledge. In the twentieth century, however, the optimism of the secular philosophers has all but disappeared. They despair of knowledge.

Like their secular counterparts, the great theologians and doctors of the church taught that knowledge is possible to man. Yet the theologians of the twentieth century have repudiated that belief. They also despair of knowledge. This radical skepticism has filtered down from the philosophers and theologians and penetrated our entire culture, from television to music to literature. *The Christian in the twentieth century is confronted with an overwhelming cultural consensus—sometimes stated explicitly, but most often implicitly: Man does not and cannot know anything truly.*

What does this have to do with Christianity? Simply this: If man can know nothing truly, man can truly know nothing. We cannot know that the Bible is the Word of God, that Christ died for the sins of his people, or that Christ is alive today at the right hand of the Father. Unless knowledge is possible, Christianity is nonsensical, for it claims to be knowledge. What is at stake in the twentieth century is not simply a single doctrine, such as the Virgin Birth, or the existence of hell, as important as those doctrines may be, but the whole of Christianity itself. If knowledge is not possible to man, it is worse than silly to argue points of doctrine—it is insane.

The irrationalism of the present age is so thorough-going and pervasive that even the Remnant—the segment of the professing church that remains faithful—has accepted much of it, frequently without even being aware of what it was accepting. In some circles this irrationalism has become synonymous with piety and humility, and those who oppose it are denounced as rationalists—as though to be logical were a sin. Our contemporary anti-theologians make a contradiction and call it a Mystery. The faithful ask for truth and are given Paradox. If any balk at swallowing the absurdities of the anti-theologians, they are frequently marked as heretics or schismatics who seek to act independently of God.

There is no greater threat facing the true Church of Christ at this moment than the irrationalism that now controls our entire culture. Totalitarianism, guilty of tens of millions of murders, including those of millions of Christians, is to be feared, but not nearly so much as the idea that we do not and cannot know the truth. Hedonism, the popular philosophy of America, is not to be feared so much as the belief that logic— that "mere human logic," to use the religious irrationalists' own phrase—is futile. The attacks on truth, on revelation, on the intellect, and on logic are renewed daily. But note well: The misologists—the haters of logic—use logic to demonstrate the futility of using logic. The anti-intellectuals construct intricate intellectual arguments to prove the insufficiency of the intellect. The anti-theologians use the revealed Word of God to show that there can be no revealed Word of God—or that if there could, it would remain impenetrable darkness and Mystery to our finite minds.

Nonsense Has Come

Is it any wonder that the world is grasping at straws—the straws of experientialism, mysticism and drugs? After all, if people are told that the Bible contains insoluble mysteries, then is not a flight into mysticism to be expected? On what grounds can it be condemned? Certainly not on logical grounds or Biblical grounds, if logic is futile and the Bible unintelligible. Moreover, if it cannot be condemned on logical or Biblical grounds, it cannot be condemned at all. If people are going to have a religion of the mysterious, they will not adopt Christianity: They will have a genuine mystery religion. "Those who call for Nonsense," C.S. Lewis once wrote, "will find that it comes." And that is precisely what has happened. The popularity of Eastern mysticism, of drugs, and of religious experience is the logical consequence of the irrationalism of the twentieth century. There can and will be no Christian revival—and no reconstruction of society—unless and until the irrationalism of the age is totally repudiated by Christians.

The Church Defenseless

Yet how shall they do it? The spokesmen for Christianity have been fatally infected with irrationalism. The seminaries, which annually train thousands of men to teach millions of Christians, are the finishing schools of irrationalism, completing the job begun by the government schools and colleges. Some of the pulpits of the most conservative churches (we are not speaking of the apostate churches) are occupied by graduates of the anti-theological schools. These products of modern anti-theological education, when asked to give a reason for the hope that is in them, can generally respond with only the intellectual analogue of a shrug—a mumble about Mystery. They have not grasped—and therefore cannot teach those for whom they are responsible—the first truth: "And ye shall know the truth." Many, in fact, explicitly deny it, saying that, at best, we possess only "pointers" to the truth, or something "similar" to the truth, a mere analogy. Is the impotence of the Christian Church a puzzle? Is the fascination with pentecostalism and faith healing among members of conservative churches an enigma? Not when one understands the sort of studied nonsense that is purveyed in the name of God in the seminaries.

The Trinity Foundation

The creators of The Trinity Foundation firmly believe that theology is too important to be left to the licensed theologians —the graduates of the schools of theology. They have created The Trinity Foundation for the express purpose of teaching the faithful all that the Scriptures contain—not warmed over, baptized, secular philosophies. Each member of the board of directors of The Trinity Foundation has signed this oath: "I believe that the Bible alone and the Bible in its entirety is the Word of God and, therefore, inerrant in the autographs. I believe that the system of truth presented in the Bible is best summarized in the Westminster Confession of Faith. So help me God."

The ministry of The Trinity Foundation is the presentation of the system of truth taught in Scripture as clearly and as completely as possible. We do not regard obscurity as a virtue, nor confusion as a sign of spirituality. Confusion, like all error, is sin, and teaching that confusion is all that Christians can hope for is doubly sin.

The presentation of the truth of Scripture necessarily involves the rejection of error. The Foundation has exposed and will continue to expose the irrationalism of the twentieth century, whether its current spokesman be an existentialist philosopher or a professed Reformed theologian. We oppose anti-intellectualism, whether it be espoused by a neo-orthodox theologian or a fundamentalist evangelist. We reject misology, whether it be on the lips of a neo-evangelical or those of a Roman Catholic charismatic. To each error we bring the brilliant light of Scripture, proving all things, and holding fast to that which is true.

The Primacy of Theory

The ministry of The Trinity Foundation is not a "practical" ministry. If you are a pastor, we will not enlighten you on how to organize an ecumenical prayer meeting in your community or how to double church attendance in a year. If you are a homemaker, you will have to read elsewhere to find out how to become a total woman. If you are a businessman, we will not tell you how to develop a social conscience. The professing church is drowning in such "practical" advice.

The Trinity Foundation is unapologetically theoretical in its outlook, believing that theory without practice is dead, and that practice without theory is blind. The trouble with the professing church is not primarily in its practice, but in its theory. Christians do not know, and many do not even care to know, the doctrines of Scripture. Doctrine is intellectual, and Christians are generally anti-intellectual. Doctrine is ivory tower philosophy, and they scorn ivory towers. The ivory tower, however, is the control tower of a civilization. It is a fundamental, theoretical mistake of the practical men to think that they can be merely practical, for practice is always the practice of some theory. The relationship between theory and practice is the relationship between cause and effect. If a person believes correct theory, his practice will tend to be correct. The practice of contemporary Christians is immoral because it is the practice of false theories. It is a major theoretical mistake of the practical men to think that they can ignore the ivory towers of the philosophers and theologians as irrelevant to their lives. Every action that the "practical" men take is governed by the thinking that has occurred in some ivory tower—whether that tower be the British Museum, the Academy, a home in Basel, Switzerland, or a tent in Israel.

In Understanding Be Men

It is the first duty of the Christian to understand correct theory—correct doctrine—and thereby implement correct practice. This order—first theory, then practice—is both logical and Biblical. It is, for example, exhibited in Paul's epistle to the

Romans, in which he spends the first eleven chapters expounding theory and the last five discussing practice. The contemporary teachers of Christians have not only reversed the order, they have inverted the Pauline emphasis on theory and practice. The virtually complete failure of the teachers of the professing church to instruct the faithful in correct doctrine is the cause of the misconduct and cultural impotence of Christians. The Church's lack of power is the result of its lack of truth. The *Gospel* is the power of God, not religious experience or personal relationship. The Church has no power because it has abandoned the Gospel, the good news, for a religion of experientialism. Twentieth century American Christians are children carried about by every wind of doctrine, not knowing what they believe, or even if they believe anything for certain.

The chief purpose of The Trinity Foundation is to counteract the irrationalism of the age and to expose the errors of the teachers of the church. Our emphasis—on the Bible as the sole source of truth, on the primacy of the intellect, on the supreme importance of correct doctrine, and on the necessity for systematic and logical thinking—is almost unique in Christendom. To the extent that the church survives—and she will survive and flourish—it will be because of her increasing acceptance of these basic ideas and their logical implications.

We believe that the Trinity Foundation is filling a vacuum in Christendom. We are saying that Christianity is intellectually defensible—that, in fact, it is the only intellectually defensible system of thought. We are saying that God has made the wisdom of this world—whether that wisdom be called science, religion, philosophy, or common sense—foolishness. We are appealing to all Christians who have not conceded defeat in the intellectual battle with the world to join us in our efforts to raise a standard to which all men of sound mind can repair.

The love of truth, of God's Word, has all but disappeared in our time. We are committed to and pray for a great instauration. But though we may not see this reformation of Christendom in our lifetimes, we believe it is our duty to present the whole counsel of God because Christ has commanded it. The results of our teaching are in God's hands, not ours. Whatever those results, his Word is never taught in vain, but always accomplishes the result that he intended it to accomplish. Professor Gordon H. Clark has stated our view well:

> There have been times in the history of God's people, for example, in the days of Jeremiah, when refreshing grace and widespread revival were not to be expected: the time was one of chastisement. If this twentieth century is of a similar nature, individual Christians here and there can find comfort and strength in a study of God's Word. But if God has decreed happier days for us and if we may expect a world-shaking and genuine spiritual awakening, then it is the author's belief that a zeal for souls, however necessary, is not the sufficient condition. Have there not been devout saints in every age, numerous enough to carry on a revival? Twelve such persons are plenty. What distinguishes the arid ages from the period of the Reformation, when nations were moved as they had not been since Paul preached in Ephesus, Corinth, and Rome, is the latter's fullness of knowledge of God's Word. To echo an early Reformation thought, when the ploughman and the garage attendant know the Bible as well as the theologian does, and know it better than some contemporary theologians, then the desired awakening shall have already occurred.

In addition to publishing books, of which *Sanctification* is the thirty-third, the Foundation publishes a monthly newsletter, *The Trinity Review*. Subscriptions to *The Review* are free; please write to the address below to become a subscriber. If you would like further information or would like to join us in our work, please let us know.

The Trinity Foundation is a non-profit foundation tax-exempt under section 501 (c)(3) of the Internal Revenue Code of 1954. You can help us disseminate the Word of God through your tax-deductible contributions to the Foundation.

And we know that the Son of God is come, and hath given us an understanding, that we may know him that is true, and we are in him that is true, in his Son Jesus Christ. This is the true God, and eternal life.

John W. Robbins

Intellectual Ammunition

The Trinity Foundation is committed to the reconstruction of philosophy and theology along Biblical lines. We regard God's command to bring all our thoughts into conformity with Christ very seriously, and the books listed below are designed to accomplish that goal. They are written with two subordinate purposes: (1) to demolish all secular claims to knowledge; and (2) to build a system of truth based upon the Bible alone.

Philosophy

Behaviorism and Christianity, Gordon H. Clark $6.95
Behaviorism *is a critique of both secular and religious behaviorists. It includes chapters on John Watson, Edgar S. Singer Jr., Gilbert Ryle, B.F. Skinner, and Donald MacKay. Clark's refutation of behaviorism and his argument for a Christian doctrine of man are unanswerable.*

A Christian Philosophy of Education, Gordon H. Clark $8.95
The first edition of this book was published in 1946. It sparked the contemporary interest in Christian schools. Dr. Clark has thoroughly revised and updated it, and it is needed now more than ever. Its chapters include: The Need for a World-View, The Christian World-View, The Alternative to Christian Theism, Neutrality, Ethics, The Christian Philosophy of Education, Academic Matters, Kindergarten to University. Three appendices are included as well: The Relationship of Public Education to Christianity, A Protestant World-View, and Art and the Gospel.

A Christian View of Men and Things, Gordon H. Clark $10.95
No other book achieves what A Christian View *does: the presentation of Christianity as it applies to history, politics, ethics, science, religion, and epistemology. Clark's command of both worldly philosophy and Scripture is evident on every page, and the result is a breathtaking and invigorating challenge to the wisdom of this world.*

Clark Speaks From The Grave, Gordon H. Clark $3.95
Dr. Clark chides some of his critics for their failure to defend Christianity competently. Clark Speaks *is a stimulating and illuminat- discussion of ᵗhe errors of contemporary apologists.*

Education, Christianity, and the State $7.95
J. Gresham Machen
Machen was one of the foremost educators, theologians, and defenders of Christianity in the twentieth century. The author of numerous scholarly books, Machen saw clearly that if Christianity is to survive and flourish, a system of Christian grade schools must be established. This collection of essays captures his thought on education over nearly three decades.

Essays on Ethics and Politics $10.95
Gordon H. Clark
Clark's s essays, written over the course of five decades, are a major statement of Christian ethics.

Gordon H. Clark: Personal Recollections $6.95
John W. Robbins, editor
Friends of Dr. Clark have written their recollections of the man. Contributors include family members, colleagues, students, and friends such as Harold Lindsell, Carl Henry, Ronald Nash, Dwight Zeller, and Mary Crumpacker. The book includes an extensive bibliography of Clark's work.

John Dewey, Gordon H. Clark $2.00
America has not produced many philosophers, but John Dewey has been extremely influential. Clark examines his philosophy of Instrumentalism.

Logic, Gordon H. Clark $8.95

Written as a textbook for Christian schools, Logic *is another unique book from Clark's pen. His presentation of the laws of thought, which must be followed if Scripture is to be understood correctly, and which are found in Scripture itself, is both clear and thorough.* Logic *is an indispensable book for the thinking Christian.*

The Philosophy of Science and Belief in God $5.95
Gordon H. Clark

In opposing the contemporary idolatry of science, Clark analyzes three major aspects of science: the problem of motion, Newtonian science, and modern theories of physics. His conclusion is that science, while it may be useful, is always false; and he demonstrates its falsity in numerous ways. Since science is always false, it can offer no objection to the Bible and Christianity.

Religion, Reason and Revelation, Gordon H. Clark $7.95

One of Clark's apologetical masterpieces, Religion, Reason and Revelation *has been praised for the clarity of its thought and language. It includes chapters on Is Christianity a Religion? Faith and Reason, Inspiration and Language, Revelation and Morality, and God and Evil. It is must reading for all serious Christians.*

Thales to Dewey: A History of Philosophy paper $11.95
Gordon H. Clark hardback $16.95

This volume is the best one volume history of philosophy in English.

Three Types of Religious Philosophy, Gordon H. Clark $6.95

In this book on apologetics, Clark examines empiricism, rationalism, dogmatism, and contemporary irrationalism, which does not rise to the level of philosophy. He offers a solution to the question, "How can Christianity be defended before the world?"

Theology

The Atonement, Gordon H. Clark $8.95
This is a major addition to Clark's multi-volume systematic theology. In The Atonement, *Clark discusses the Covenants, the Virgin Birth and Incarnation, federal headship and representation, the relationship between God's sovereignty and justice, and much more. He analyzes traditional views of the Atonement and criticizes them in the light of Scripture alone.*

The Biblical Doctrine of Man, Gordon H. Clark $6.95
Is man soul and body or soul, spirit, and body? What is the image of God? Is Adam's sin imputed to his children? Is evolution true? Are men totally depraved? What is the heart? These are some of the questions discussed and answered from Scripture in this book.

Cornelius Van Til: The Man and The Myth $2.45
John W. Robbins
The actual teachings of this eminent Philadelphia theologian have been obscured by the myths that surround him. This book penetrates those myths and criticizes Van Til's surprisingly unorthodox views of God and the Bible.

Faith and Saving Faith, Gordon H. Clark $6.95
The views of the Roman Catholic church, John Calvin, Thomas Manton, John Owen, Charles Hodge, and B.B. Warfield are discussed in this book. Is the object of faith a person or a proposition? Is faith more than belief? Is belief more than thinking with assent, as Augustine said? In a world chaotic with differing views of faith, Clark clearly explains the Biblical view of faith and saving faith.

God's Hammer: The Bible and Its Critics $6.95
Gordon H. Clark
The starting point of Christianity, the doctrine on which all other doctrines depend, is "The Bible alone is the Word of God written, and therefore inerrant in the autographs." Over the centuries the opponents of Christianity, with Satanic shrewdness, have concentrated their attacks on

the truthfulness and completeness of the Bible. In the twentieth century the attack is not so much in the fields of history and archaeology as in philosophy. Clark's brilliant defense of the complete truthfulness of the Bible is captured in this collection of eleven major essays.

Guide to the Westminster Confession and Catechism $13.95
James E. Bordwine

This large book contains the full text of both the Westminster Confession (both original and American versions) and the Larger Catechism. In addition, it offers a chapter-by-chapter summary of the Confession and a unique index to both the Confession and the Catechism.

The Incarnation, Gordon H. Clark $8.95

Who was Christ? The attack on the Incarnation in the nineteenth and twentieth centuries has been vigorous, but the orthodox response has been lame. Clark reconstructs the doctrine of the Incarnation building and improving upon the Chalcedonian definition.

In Defense of Theology, Gordon H. Clark $9.95

There are four groups to whom Clark addresses this book: the average Christians who are uninterested in theology, the atheists and agnostics, the religious experientialists, and the serious Christians. The vindication of the knowledge of God against the objections of three of these groups is the first step in theology.

The Johannine Logos, Gordon H. Clark $5.95

Clark analyzes the relationship between Christ, who is the truth, and the Bible. He explains why John used the same word to refer to both Christ and his teaching. Chapters deal with the Prologue to John's Gospel, Logos and Rheemata, Truth, and Saving Faith.

Logical Criticisms of Textual Criticism $3.25
Gordon H. Clark

In this critique of the science of textual criticism, Dr. Clark exposes the fallacious argumentation of the modern textual critics and defends the view that the early Christians knew better than the modern critics which manuscripts of the New Testament were more accurate.

Pat Robertson: A Warning to America, John W. Robbins $6.95
The Protestant Reformation was based on the Biblical principle that the Bible is the only revelation from God, yet a growing religious movement, led by Pat Robertson, asserts that God speaks to them directly. This book addresses the serious issue of religious fanaticism in America by examining the theological views of Pat Robertson.

Predestination, Gordon H. Clark $8.95
Clark thoroughly discusses one of the most controversial and pervasive doctrines of the Bible: that God is, quite literally, Almighty. Free will, the origin of evil, God's omniscience, creation, and the new birth are all presented within a Scriptural framework. The objections of those who do not believe in the Almighty God are considered and refuted. This edition also contains the text of the booklet, Predestination in the Old Testament.

Sanctification, Gordon H. Clark $8.95
In this book, which is part of Clark's multi-volume systematic theology, he discusses historical theories of sanctification, the sacraments, and the Biblical doctrine of sanctification.

Scripture Twisting in the Seminaries. Part 1: Feminism $5.95
John W. Robbins
An analysis of the views of three graduates of Westminster Seminary on the role of women in the church.

Today's Evangelism: Counterfeit or Genuine? $6.95
Gordon H. Clark
Clark compares the methods and messages of today's evangelists with Scripture, and finds that Christianity is on the wane because the Gospel has been distorted or lost. This is an extremely useful and enlightening book.

The Trinity, Gordon H. Clark $8.95
Apart from the doctrine of Scripture, no teaching of the Bible is more important than the doctrine of God. Clark's defense of the orthodox doctrine of the Trinity is a principal portion of a major new work of Systematic Theology now in progress. There are chapters on the deity of Christ,

Augustine, the incomprehensibility of God, Bavinck and Van Til, and the Holy Spirit, among others.

What Do Presbyterians Believe? Gordon H. Clark $7.95
    This classic introduction to Christian doctrine has been republished. It is the best commentary on the Westminster Confession of Faith that has ever been written.

Commentaries on the New Testament

Colossians, Gordon H. Clark $6.95
Ephesians, Gordon H. Clark $8.95
First Corinthians, Gordon H. Clark $10.95
First John, Gordon H. Clark $10.95
First and Second Thessalonians, Gordon H. Clark $5.95
The Pastoral Epistles (I and II Timothy and Titus) $9.95
    Gordon H. Clark
    All of Clark's commentaries are expository, not technical, and are written for the Christian layman. His purpose is to explain the text clearly and accurately so that the Word of God will be thoroughly known by every Christian.

The Trinity Library

We will send you one copy of each of the 36 books listed above for the low price of $175. The regular price of these books is $275. You may also order the books you want individually on the order blank on the next page. Because some of the books are in short supply, we must reserve the right to substitute others of equal or greater value in The Trinity Library. This special offer expires June 30, 1994.

Order Form

Name _____

Address _____

_____

Please: □ add my name to the mailing list for *The Trinity Review* I understand that there is no charge for the *Review*

□ accept my tax deductible contribution of $ _____ for the work of the Foundation.

□ send me _____ copies of *Sanctification.* I enclose as payment $ _____.

□ send me the Trinity Library of 36 books. I enclose $175 as full payment for it.

□ send me the following books. I enclose full payment in the amount of $ _____ for them.

_____

_____

_____

_____

_____

_____

_____

Mail to: **The Trinity Foundation**
Post Office Box 700
Jefferson, MD 21755

Please add $2.50 for postage on orders less than $10. Thank you.
For quantity discounts, please write to the Foundation.